FALCKNER'S *CURIEUSE NACHRICHT VON PENSYLVANIA*

METALMARK BOOKS

WILLIAM PENN
ÆTAT 52

FALCKNER'S

Curieuse Nachricht

Von

PENSYLVANIA

THE BOOK THAT STIMULATED THE GREAT

German Emigration

TO

Pennsylvania

IN THE EARLY YEARS OF THE XVIII CENTURY.

A Reprint of the Edition of 1702, amplified with the Text of the Original Manuscript in the Halle Archives. Together with an Introduction and English Translation of the Complete Work

BY

Julius Friedrich Sachse, Litt.D.

Member American Philosophical Society —Historical Society of Pennsylvania—
Pennsylvania-German Society—American Historical Association—
International Congress of Orientalists, etc., etc.

Philadelphia :
PRINTED FOR THE AUTHOR
MDCCCCV

Reprinted from

Volume XIV., Proceedings of the Pennsylvania–German Society

———————

Edition limited to two hundred and fifty copies

of which this is No............................

Press of
The New Era Printing Company
Lancaster, Pa.

THIS VOLUME

IS PRINTED AS A MEMORIAL

TO THE

Early German Settlers

of

Pennsylvania

WHO LEFT THE FATHERLAND TO FOUND A HOME
FOR THEMSELVES AND POSTERITY

IN

Penn's Province

WHERE LIBERTY OF CONSCIENCE WAS ASSURED AND WHOSE
DESCENDENTS ARE NOW TO BE FOUND PROMINENT FACTORS
IN EVERY STATE OF THE AMERICAN UNION

CONTENTS.

INTRODUCTION.

CHAPTER I.

FOREWORD.

CHAPTER II.

PENN'S PROVINCE.

CHAPTER III.

FRANCIS DANIEL PASTORIUS.

CHAPTER IV.

" CURIEUSE NACHRICHT VON PENSYLVANIEN."

CHAPTER V.

DANIEL FALCKNER.

CHAPTER VI.

AUGUST HERMANN FRANCKE.

FALCKNER'S AUTHENTIC TIDINGS.

LIST OF QUESTIONS.

PRÆMONITIO.

PREFACE.

QUESTIONS 1–8.

THE VOYAGE.

ILLUSTRATIONS.

PLATES.

ILLUSTRATIONS IN TEXT.

NOTE. — The Head and Tail Pieces used in the body of the book, pp.
45 to 245, are reproductions of the Edition of 1702.

FOREWORD.

NO incident connected with the settlement of the grand old Commonwealth of Pennsylvania has aroused greater interest in the minds of the historian and the student than the migration of the German masses from the Fatherland to Penn's province on the Delaware, beginning during the reign of King Charles the Second and extending with more or less regularity, according to the political and religious conditions of Western Germany, down to the early years of the third George. It was a tide of brawn and muscle, which sought to escape the persecutions at home, and here in the new world to found homes for themselves, their families and posterity, and erect in the wilderness altars for the worship of Almighty God, according to the dictates of their conscience, free and untrammelled by any ecclesiastical or secular restrictions.

The story of the two great migrations from Germany to Pennsylvania in 1709 and 1764 has been told in detail.

The first one, known as the *Massen auswanderung* or
" Exodus of 1709 " is exhaustively set forth in the seventh
volume of the Proceedings of the Pennsylvania-German
Society. That of the second great migration, in the year
1764, will be found upon the pages of the Lutheran
Church Review for the year 1903 and was compiled from
original sources and documents by the present writer.

Full and instructive accounts of the continuous general
movement of the Germans to Pennsylvania are presented
in the contributions to our history by fellow members of
the Pennsylvania-German Society and printed in the proceedings of that organization.

It is not our present purpose to go over any of the ground
already covered by the above investigators, but to bring to
notice some new and additional matter, and direct attention to the factor that set this great migratory stream in
motion, one which has had so great and salutatory an
effect upon the development, not only of Pennsylvania,
but of the whole United States, which is now justly known
as the great world power of the western hemisphere.

This great factor is nothing less than a small duodecimo,
but little known except to historians and collectors of rare
books. So scarce is this little volume that it is seldom
quoted by dealers in their lists of Americana or found in
the *antiquariat* catalogues of Germany. In the only instance of the latter known to the writer the book was
quoted at 250 marks, a sum equivalent to $62.50 of our
money.

Of the few known copies, one is in the collection of the
Historical Society of Pennsylvania; and others in that of
the old German Society, Philadelphia Library Company,
and in the collection of an ex-president of the Pennsylvania-German Society.

Heretofore nothing was known as to the conditions under which this book was written and published or who propounded the 103 questions, the answers to which, besides giving advice to the prospective emigrant and settler, present an insight into the life and habits of the Indians and the social conditions of Penn's Colony in its infancy, not to be found elsewhere.

It was the good fortune of the writer, during his late search among the archives in the Fatherland, after records and material bearing upon the early history of this province, to find not only the original manuscript of this book, but also the original set of questions, as submitted to Daniel Falckner, the learned scholar and Pietist who had lately returned from the solitudes of the hermitage on the Wissahickon. This set of questions proved to be in the handwriting of no less a person than the celebrated divine and scholar, August Hermann Francke, who together with Spener was then at the head of the Pietistical movement in the Lutheran Church in Germany.

A careful copy of this manuscript was made for the writer. This has since been compared with the printed version, which it appears differs slightly in some of its minor particulars from the original. Then again a few additions were made to the text, while a considerable portion of the prologue and text was omitted. The main features, however, remain the same in both versions. The account, as will be shown, went through several editions, which were issued simultaneously in Leipzig and Frankfort-on-the-Mayn.

CHAPTER II.

THE PROVINCE OF PENNSYLVANIA.

PENNSYLVANIA was the best advertised province of all the original thirteen Colonies, and it was mainly due to the liberal use of printer's ink that the stream of emigration was aroused, and set in so strongly and steadily towards King Charles the Second's grant to William Penn, at a time when emigration to the New World was lagging. No professional promoter or land speculator of the present day could have devised any scheme which would have proved a greater success than the means taken by William Penn and his counsellor Benjamin Furly to advertise his province among the various nations and conditions of men. It is quite piquant to picture the Society of Friends as the founders of American advertising. But such they were.

By a reference to the list of title-pages printed in facsimile in Volume VII., Proceedings of the Pennsylvania-

German Society, it will be seen that no less than fifty-eight books, broadsides, and pamphlets, in English, Dutch, German and French are enumerated which bear upon the early settlement of Pennsylvania.

The first four of these are by Penn and Furly, and are of a religious nature. We then come to William Penn's *Some Account of the Province of Pennsylvania in America.* This account was compiled by Penn and Furly from the best information then obtainable, and printed almost immediately after the grant received the royal confirmation in the year 1681. It was issued in English, German and Dutch, and was liberally circulated by Furly throughout Holland and the country adjacent to the Rhine.

The pamphlet begins with a glowing account of the new province, setting forth the advantages offered by it to the husbandman and tiller of the soil. By way of comparison, Penn says that an improved acre in the Barbadoes is worth three times the value of an acre in England, and that in Virginia an acre of tobacco pays a clear profit of twenty-five pounds, besides twenty barrels of corn yearly. Thence Penn proceeds, as he states, "to give some account of his concerns." This section he divides under the following five heads :

1. I shall say what may be necessary of the place or province.

2. Touch upon the constitutions.

3. Lay down the conditions.

4. Give my sense of what persons will be fit to go.

5. What utensils, furniture and commodities are fit to carry with them, with the charge of the voyage, and what is first to be done and expected there for some time.

Then follows an abstract of the grant by King Charles II., closing with an invocation, in which Penn says:

"I beseech Almighty God to direct us, that his blessing may attend our honest endeavour, and then the consequence of all our undertaking will turn to the glory of his great name and the true happiness of us and our posterity."

The whole matter formed a folio pamphlet of ten pages. This "Account" was at once translated by Benjamin Furly into German and Dutch. The former was printed by Cunraden at Amsterdam, the Dutch version by Wynbrugge at Rotterdam. This was the earliest notice of Pennsylvania in German, and was reprinted two years later (1683) at Leipzig. To both of these translations, Furly, further to strengthen Penn's claims to German and Dutch recognition and to stimulate emigration from those countries, added a translation of Penn's "Liberty of Conscience." It was also reprinted in the *Diarium Europaeum.*

About the same time (1681) an enlarged German version of *Du Val's Universal Geography* was issued by Froberg of Nürnberg, giving some notice of Pennsylvania; and also a French book, by Reinier Leers, at Rotterdam, which mentions Pennsylvania upon the title-page.

By the aid of Furly's commercial and personal correspondents this literature was circulated throughout the Low Countries and in Germany, as far as Lübeck and Dantzic in the East and down the Rhine among the Palatines even into Switzerland.

The first practical results from these advertisements are shown by the conveyance on March 10, 1682, of 15,000 acres of land in Pennsylvania to Jacob Telner, Dirck Sip-

man of Crefeld and Jan Streypers of Kaldkirchen. These men were the first of the original Crefeld purchasers.

Shortly afterwards (1682) Penn issued another advertisement of his province. It was a pamphlet of three and a half pages, two columns to a page, the object of which was to furnish information for prospective settlers of the different nationalities.

The heading of the English version sets forth :

Information and Direction to Such Persons as are inclined to America, More Especially Those related to the Province of Pennsylvania.

This was also translated and issued in both German and Dutch. No German copy of this rare pamphlet is known, but a Dutch copy, lacking the last page and the imprint, was found among the Penn papers in the collection of the Pennsylvania Historical Society. It is endorsed : " Dutch information over Pennsylv."

Another Dutch edition of this pamphlet, with a somewhat different heading, was issued in 1686.

In the meantime Penn had printed the *Articles, settlement and offices of the free Society of Traders in Pennsylvania;* also his *Frame of the Government of the Province,* etc., neither of which appear to have been translated into any other language.

These issues were quickly followed by Penn's *Brief account of the Province of Pennsylvania,* which was at once translated and published by Furly in Dutch, French and German. This was supplemented with *Plantation work, the work of this Generation,* which however does not appear to have been issued in any but the English tongue.

Such was the literature that was being scattered broadcast throughout the different countries to bring the province

into notice, during the eighteen months that Penn had been
in possession of his charter.

While Furly was bending his efforts to induce emigration to Penn's province chiefly among the non-orthodox
sects, such as Sectarians and Separatists in Holland and
Germany, Penn was completing his arrangements for going
to his province.   He finally sailed on the *Welcome* in
August, 1682, arriving at New Castle on the Delaware on
October 27, after a voyage of fifty-four days.

BENJAMIN FURLY.

B. APRIL 13, 1636; D. MARCH, 1714.

CHAPTER III.

Francis Daniel Pastorius.

A YEAR later, August 16, 1683, Francis Daniel Pastorius arrived at Philadelphia. He came out as the representative of a number of German Pietists who had acquired considerable tracts of land from Penn. Two months later he was followed by the first German settlers from Krisheim and Crefeld, who arrived in the *Concord*, October 6, 1683.

Up to this time the narratives and descriptions of the country were derived from verbal accounts and hearsay, obtained from diverse sources which were deemed by Penn and Furly to be reliable. The advent of Penn, Pastorius, the Crefelders and other settlers brought forth a new set of letters and authentic descriptions, direct from the New

World, giving personal experiences and accounts derived
from actual observation.

This class of literature was destined to attract greater
attention than the vague accounts heretofore published,
and thus gradually to stimulate German emigration.

Francis Daniel Pastorius.

These missives were not all printed immediately, but
were transcribed as soon as received by Furly, and copies
were sent to leading Pietists and Sectarians in Germany
and Holland who were interested in promoting the settlement of Pennsylvania, a colony where liberty of conscience
was assured. Some of these persons in turn made new
copies thereof, either in whole or in part, for their own use
before passing the original transcript to others who were
interested. Thus was the information of Penn's colony
in its earliest days spread in the non-orthodox circles quickly
and quietly.

It was the good fortune of the writer, in one of his pil-
grimages to the Fatherland, to discover in the Ministerial
archives of Lübeck one of these manuscript volumes relat-
ing to the early settlement of Penn's province. These copies
were made by one Jaspar Balthasar Könneken, a book-
seller of Lübeck (d. 1715) scholar and Pietist, an intimate
associate of the members who formed the Frankfort Company. Könneken, as correspondent of Furly, took great
interest in the settlement of Pennsylvania, and was only
dissuaded from going out in 1683 or joining the colony on
the Wissahickon in 1694 on account of his advanced age.

He carefully copied and preserved the information sent
him by Furly. Here we find:

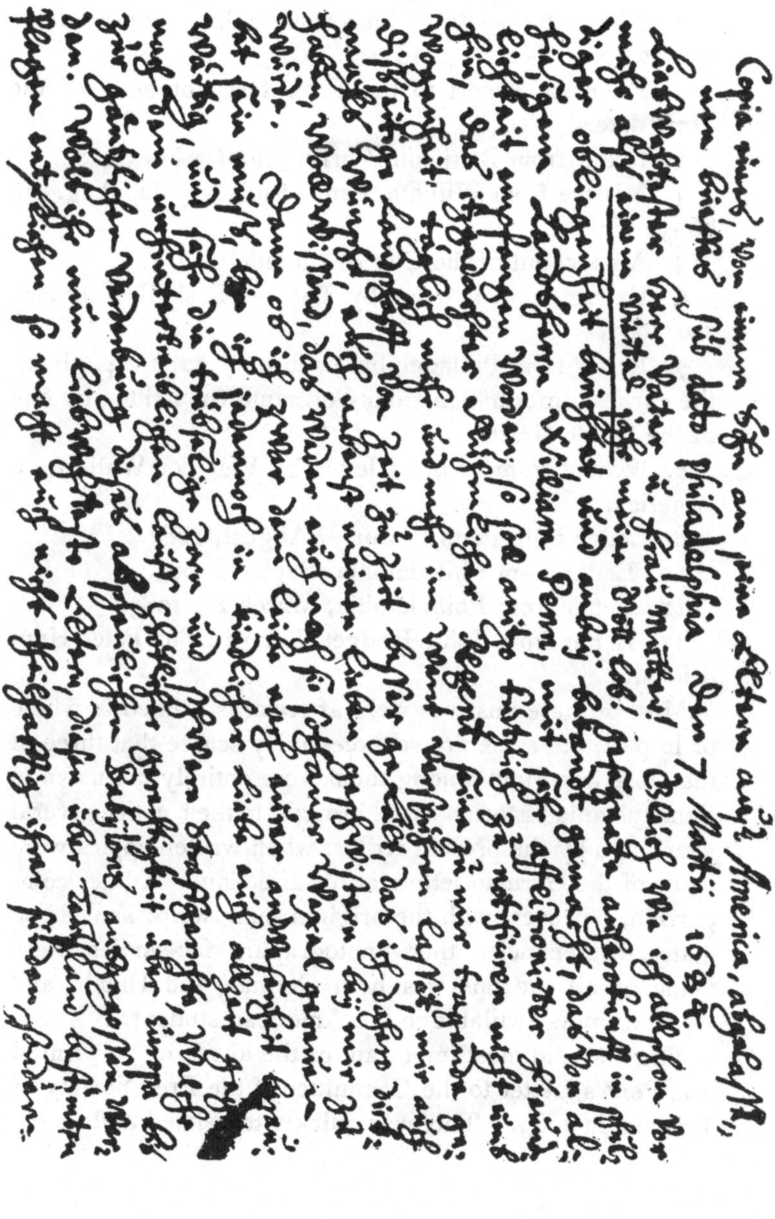

SPECIMEN PAGE OF THE KÖNNEKEN MANUSCRIPT IN THE LÜBECK ARCHIVES.

1. The letter sent by Pastorius to his parents, dated Philadelphia, March 7, 1684.

2. Pastorius' report to the Frankfort Company of the same date.

3. Letter from Benjamin Furly, 5th of 3 Mo., 1684.

4. Missive from William Penn, Philadelphia, Aug. 26, 1683.

5. An account of the City of Philadelphia.

6. Extract from a letter by Thomas Paskell, February 10, 1683.

7. Letter from Philadelphia, February 12, 1684, giving the earliest information from Germantown, written by one of the Op de Graffs.

8. Extract from an open letter by Van der Walle from America.

9. Letter from Penn to Furly, August, 1683.

10. Letter from Philadelphia, Sept. 1, 1683.

11. Letter from Philadelphia, March 27, 1683.

12. Letter from John Rodger Langwart to Peter Hendricks.

Most of these missives were afterwards printed in whole or in part, but some are so excessively scarce that three of the most important among them were entirely unknown to Pennsylvania historians until brought to their notice several years ago by the present writer, when written copies were made of the German letters at his direction. A later comparison, however, with the original manuscript showed so many discrepancies that photographic fac-similes were made of all the missives both German and Dutch, and these are now available to the American student.

The first and most important of the above to be printed was Penn's Letter to the Committee of the Free Society of Traders, in 1683. This was quickly translated and issued

in Low Dutch, German and French. To these were added Holmes' Description of Philadelphia and Thomas Paskel's letter of February 10, 1683. A second edition of the Dutch version was published in 1684, as is shown by the Könneken manuscript. This publication was followed a year later by another advertisement by Penn, known as *A further account of the Province.* This was also printed in the Continental tongues.

Next we have Pastorius' two missives, numbers one and two on the above list:[1]

(1) *Copia eines, von einem Sohn an seine Eltern aus America abgelassenen Brieffes. Sub. Dato Philadelphia den 7 Martii, 1684.*

(2) *Sichere Nachricht aus Amerika, wegen der Landschafft Pennsylvanien, von einen dorthin gereisten Deutschen. Sub. dato 7 Martii, 1684.*

We also have two missives in Low Dutch, one from Joris Wertmuller, a Switzer, dated Germantown, March 16, 1684, the other from Cornelius Bom, a cake baker, dated Philadelphia, October 12, 1684.[2] These two letters were published by Pieter Van Wÿnbrugge at Rotterdam, and are undoubtedly the first accounts from actual German or Dutch settlers to be published. The above mentioned Pastorius missives not having been printed until the following year, the title reads as follows:

Twee Missiven geschreven uyt Pennsylvania a' Ene door een Hollander woonachtig in Philadelfia, d' Ander door Switzer, woonachtig in German Town, Dat is Hoogduytse Stadt. Van den 16, Maert, 1684. Nieuwen Stijl. tot Rotterdam, anno 1684.

---

[1] Both of these missives are reproduced in facsimile and translation in Sachse's "Letters from Germantown, 1683-1684." Lübeck and Philadelphia, 1903.

[2] For translation of these two missives see Pennypacker's "Hendrick Pannebecker, 1674-1754," pp. 27-39.

◄§(1)§►

Sichere Nachricht auß America, wegen der Landschafft Pennsylvania / von einem dorthin gereißten Teutschen / de dato Philadelphia, den 7. Martii 1684.

Einer schuldigen Obliegenheit so wol als auch meinem Abschiedlichen Versprechen ein Gnügen zu leisten/sol ich etwas umbständlicher advisiren, wie und was ich hiesiger Landen gefunden und angemercket habe/ und weilen mir nicht unwissend./ daß durch ungleiche Relation ihrer viel hinter das Licht geführet würden / versichere ich zum vorauß/daß ich mit ohnpartheyischer Feder ohne verfälschlichen Zusatz / beedes die Ungemächlichkeiten der Reiß und den Mangel hiesiger Provintz / als den von andern fast gar zu sehr gelobten Uberfluß desselben getreulich anführen wolle : Dann ich verlange an meinem wenigen Orte mehr nicht / als zu wandeln in den Fußstapffen deß jenigen / welcher ist der Weg/ und zu folgen seinen heilsamen Lehren/ weil Er die Warheit ist/ auff daß ich unauffhörlich mit Ihm dem ewigen Leben vereinigt bleibe.

1. Ich wil also den Anfang machen von der Seefart/welche sicherlich so wol wegen der zu befürchten habender Schiffbrüche/gefährlich/als auch wegen der schlechten und harten Schiffskost/sehr beschwerlich ist/daß ich auß eigener Erfahrung nun ziemlich verstehe/was David im 107. Psalm sagt / daß man auff dem Meer nicht nur die Wunderwerck deß HErrn / sondern auch den Geist deß Ungewitters verspühren und warnehmen könne. Dann meine Anheroreiß belangend/bin ich mit 4. Knechten / 2. Mägden/ 2. Kindern und 1. Jungen/den 10. Jun. von Deal abgesegelt/ hatten den gantzen Weg über meiste is widrigen/und nicht 12. Stund aneinander favorablen Wind/viel Sturm-und Donnerwetter/auch zerbrach der vorderste Mast zu zweyen malen/so daß wir erst binnen 10. Wochen allhier arrivirt ; jedoch sat cito, si sat bene. Massen es selten geschiehet/daß einige viel zeitlicher anhero kommen. Die Crefelder/welche den 6. Octobr. allhier angelangt/waren ebenfals 10.Wochen auff der See/ und das Schiff das mit dem unsern von Deal außgefahren/war 14. Tag länger unterwegs / auch starben einige Menschen darauff. Gedachte Crefelder haben auch zwischen Roterdam und Engelland eine erwachsene Tochter verloren/welcher Verlust jedoch zwischen Engelland und Pennsilvanien mit der Geburt zweyer Kinder ersetzt worden. Auff unserm Schiff hingegen ist niemand Todes verfahren / auch niemand geboren/ꝛc. Fast alle Passagiers waren etliche Tag lang Seekranck/ich aber nicht über 4. Stund / hereutgegen war ich andern Accidentien unterworffen/da mir nemlich die zwey außgehauene Löben über unserer Schiffsloch schier den Rucken eingeschlagen / und ich den 9. Jul. bey nächtlichem Sturm so unuersehem auff die lincke Seiten gefallen/ daß ich einige Tag über deß Verts hüten muste. Diese beede Fäll erinnerten mich nachdrücklich deß ersten auff alle ihre posterität durchgetrungenen Falls unserer Ureltern / welchen sie im Paradeiß / auch vieler der jenigen / die ich in diesem Jammerthal meines exilii begangen, Per varios casus, &c   allein gepreiset sey die Vatterhand göttlicher Barmhertzigkeit / welche uns zu dicke ma's wieder auffrichtet/und zurück hält/damit wir nicht gäntzlich verfallen/in den Abgrund deß Argen, Görg Wertmüller fiel gleichmässig überauß hart/Thomas Gasper/schlug am Leib sehr auß/ die Englische Magd hatte das Rothlauff/ und Isaac Dilbreck/der sonst dem äusserlichen Ansehen nach der stärckste/lag am längsten darnieder. Hatte ich also einen kleinen Schiff-Hospital/ wiewol ich allein von den Teutschen meine Lägerstätt unter den Englischen genommen/ꝛc. Daß ein Boos-gesell unsinnig/und unser Schiff durch widerholtes anschlagen eines Wallfisches zum Zittern bewegt worden/ hab ich in meinem letztern

These publications were followed in the year 1685, with a more extended account of the Province by Cornelius Bom, and a Latin missive, descriptive of Germantown by Pastorius, dated Germantown, December 1, 1688. It was sent to Dr. Modelius, a Professor at the University of Altdorf, and intended to attract the attention of the learned classes. It was not, however, published until April, 1691, when the missive was inserted in the *Monatliche Unterredungen*, a serial published by Wilhelm Ernst Tenzel, the celebrated royal Saxon historian and author, at that time Professor at the Gotha Gymnasium. The letters, however, failed to interest the learned classes to any extent at this time, nor is it known to have been translated or republished until the year 1700 when a portion of this letter was incorporated by Pastorius in his *Beschreibung von Pennsylvanien, Contenta Literarum Francisci Danielis Pastorii, an Herrn Georg Leonhard Modeln, Rectorem Scholæ Windsheimensis*. The missive contains little that is new or of interest except the statement that within the five years past the population of Germantown has increased from 13 to 50.

" Quanquam enim anno 1683. tredecim tantum inchoaverimus, unius tamen lustri intervallo numerum excreverunt quinquagenarium."

Families, and not persons are evidently meant here, as in his letter of March 7, 1684, he states that " twelve families (consisting of forty-two persons) already live there pleasantly," etc.[3]

He also makes mention of the German version of Penn's *Account of the Province of Pennsylvania* of 1681, and that he had gathered together in one volume, prior to his

---

[3] Sachse's "Letters from Germantown, 1683-1684." Translation, p. 5, Facsimile, p. 1.

Vier kleine
Doch ungemeine
Und sehr nutzliche

Tractätlein

De omnium Sanctorum Vitis
I. De omnium Pontificum Statutis
II. De Conciliorum Decisionibus
V. De Episcopis & Patriarchis Constan-
tinopolitanis.

Das ist:

1. Von Aller Heiligen Lebens-Ubung
2. Von Aller Päpste Gesetz-Einführung
3. Von der Concilien Stritt-Sopirung.
4. Von denen Bischöffen und Patriarchen
zu Constantinopel.

Zum Grunde
Der künfftighin noch ferner darauf
zu bauen Vorhabender Warheit
præmittiret,

Durch
FRANCISCUM DANIELEM
PASTORIUN. J. U. L.

Aus der
In Pensylvania neulichst von mir in
Grund angelegten / und nun mit gutem
Succes aufgehenden Stadt:

GERMANOPOLI
Anno Christi M. DC. XC.

TITLE PAGE OF PASTORIUS' "FOUR USEFUL TRACTS."

Uytgevoerd te LEYDEN door PIETER VANDER AA met Privilegie.

A DUTCH MAP SHOWING THE SWEDISH AND DUTCH SETTLEMENTS

Engraved about 1665.

THE WEST AND EAST SIDES OF THE SOUTH (DELAWARE) RIVER.

departure from Germany, several pamphlets bearing upon
the province. These were evidently the different versions
of Penn's " Account" and other pamphlets published by
Penn and Furly to advertise the province, and for his
information and use in connection with the formation of
the Frankfort Company. [Not printed in Frankfort as
the quotation *quod Francofurti typis excriptum foras
prodiit;* has led some students to believe.]

German interest in Penn's colony gradually became
aroused, especially in mercantile and pietistical circles.
As a result we find the members of the Frankfort Company taking a more active interest in their venture, as is
shown by the celebrated agreement dated November 12,
1686.

This interest was accentuated by the publication, in 1690,
of Pastorius' *Vier Kleine doch ungemeine und sehr Nütz-
liche Tractätlein,* followed two years later (1692) with a
publication of his *Kurtze geographische Beschreibung,* appended to his father's sketch of Windsheim. This description was reprinted in various periodicals of the day.

Henceforth we have a number of German accounts and
descriptions from settlers in Pennsylvania.

CHAPTER IV.

OWING to the continued persecutions of the Pietists in Germany, the attention of such leaders as Spener and Francke was serously turned towards Pennsylvania as an asylum for German Pietists, and resulted in the sending out of the party under Magisters Kelpius, Köster and Daniel Falckner, who settled on the Wissahickon in 1694.

From thence we have one of the most interesting and instructive missives from the province, dated August 7, 1694. It was written by Johann Gottfried Seelig, a former secretary of the great Spener. The manuscript is still preserved in the archives at Halle. It was printed in 1695 and is exceedingly scarce. From this time onward we also have some controversial literature in which Köster and Pastorius figured, which was circulated in Germany and tended to advertise the Colony.

Gabriel Thomas' "Historical Account" was published in London in 1698, and was by far the largest and most pretentious history of Pennsylvania thus far attempted.

Almost simultaneously with its appearance in London it was issued in German in the interests of the Frankfort Company, and was followed in 1700 by Pastorius' *Umständige geographische Beschreiburg.* In the meantime Daniel Falckner had returned to Germany, arriving either late in 1698 or early in 1699, and reported the condition of the province to Furly at Rotterdam and to the Pietistic leaders at Halle.

While at the latter place, Rev. August Herman Francke, who was then at the head of the Pietistic movement in Germany, propounded seventy-three written questions to Daniel Falckner, relative to the voyage to America and the conditions of the country and its inhabitants, both European and Indian.

These questions were replied to by Falckner in writing in exhaustive answers, wherein he gives the results of his own experience and observations. His manuscript is prefixed with a lengthy preface or *Praemonenda*, showing that he was of the orthodox Lutheran faith. The whole closes with an extended scheme for a moral and religious communistic settlement or economy, based upon a capital of 4,000 Rix Dollars.

Later on twenty-one additional pertinent questions were propounded to him as to certain conditions in the New World. These were also answered with an equal degree of frankness. Transcripts of these questions and answers were also made and circulated similar to the Könneken MSS. The original set of questions and answers, with

Curieuse Nachricht

Von

PENSYLVANIA

in

Norden = America

Welche /

Auf Begehren guter Freunde /

Uber vorgelegte 103. Fragen / bey seiner Abreiß aus Teutschland nach obigem Lande Anno 1700. ertheilet / und nun Anno 1702 in den Druck gegeben worden.

Von

Daniel Falckner / Professore, Burgern und Pilgrim allda.

Franckfurt und Leipzig /
Zu finden bey Andreas Otto / Buchhändlern.
Im Jahr Christi 1702.

TITLE PAGE OF FALCKNER'S "ACCURATE TIDINGS."

several fragments of the transcripts, however, remained in the archives at Halle, where they were found, examined and copied, after the lapse of two hundred years, by and under the direction of the present writer.

Two years after the return to America of the Falckner brothers, as attorneys for the Frankfort Company, as well as Benjamin Furly, an edition of these questions and answers was published in the coloquial style of the period by the Frankfort Company. The printed copy as before stated differs in some particulars from the original manuscript, as some additional matter concerning the Indians was added, and the preface, which was really a religious dissertation, was greatly reduced. A translation of the title reads as follows :

"Accurate tidings from Pennsylvania in Northern America, which, at solicitation of good friends, regarding 103 propounded questions, upon his departure from Germany to the above country, anno 1700, were imparted, and now, anno 1702, are given in print, by Daniel Falckner Professor,[4] Citizen and Pilgrim in that very place." [Frankfort and Leipzig. To be found at Andreas Otto's, Publisher. In the year of Christ 1702.]

Little did either Rev. Francke or Daniel Falckner at that time realize the worth of this contribution to our history, or the factor this little book was destined to become in stimulating the German emigration ; nor could they ever have imagined the financial value placed upon a copy of this book two centuries later.

Pastorius' *Umständige Geographische Beschreibung* and Falckner's *Curieuse Nachricht* were issued in several editions. In 1704 a new edition of both was published in one volume under the title : *Continuatio der Beschreibung*

---

[4] Of Religion.

Umständige Geographische

Beschreibung

Der zu allerletzt erfundenen
Provintz

PENSYLVA-
NIÆ,

In denen End-Gräntzen
AMERICÆ
In der West = Welt gelegen
Durch
FRANCISCUM DANIELEM
PASTORIUM,
J. V. Lic. und Friedens-Richtern
daselbsten:

Worbey angehencket sind einige no-
table Begebenheiten/ und Bericht-
Schreiben an dessen Herrn
Vattern
MELCHIOREM ADAMUM
PASTORIUM,
Und andere gute Freunde.

Franckfurt und Leipzig/
Zufinden bey Andreas Otto. 1704.

TITLE PAGE OF PASTORIUS' GEOGRAPHIC DESCRIPTION.

CONTINUATIO
Der
Beſchreibung der Landſchafft
PENSYLVANIÆ
An denen End-Gräntzen
AMERICÆ.
Uber vorige des Herrn Paſtorii
Relationes.
In ſich haltend:
Die Situation, und Fruchtbarkeit des
Erdbodens. Die Schiffreiche und andere
Flüſſe. Die Anzahl derer bißhero gebauten Städte.
Die ſeltſame Creaturen an Thieren / Vögeln und Fiſchen.
Die Mineralien und Edelgeſteine　Deren eingebohrnen wilden Völcker Sprachen / Religion und Gebräuche. Und
die erſten Chriſtlichen Pflantzer und Anbauer
dieſes Landes.

Beſchrieben von
GABRIEL THOMAS
15. Jährigen Inwohner dieſes
Landes.

Welchem Tractätlein noch beygefüget ſind:
Des Hn. DANIEL FALCKNERS
Burgers und Pilgrims in Penſylvania 193.
Beantwortungen uff vorgelegte Fragen von
guten Freunden.

Franckfurt und Leipzig /
Zu finden bey Andreas Otto / Buchhändlern.

TITLE PAGE OF PASTORIUS' "CONTINUATION" TOGETHER WITH
THOMAS' AND FALCKNER'S "ACCOUNTS."

der Landschafft Pennsylvania ("Continuation of the description of the province of Pennsylvania "), to which was added a German translation of Gabriel Thomas' " Account." This combination formed the most important early work on Pennsylvania published in the German language.

It was these successive editions of Pastorius and Falckner's accounts that called the attention of the sturdy yeomanry of the Fatherland to the advantages of Penn's colony, and started that great stream of emigration which at one time almost threatened to depopulate the Palatinate, brought thousands and thousands of Germans to our province and made Pennsylvania the great Commonwealth it is to-day.

Strange how little this work of Daniel Falckner was known to historians and writers on Pennsylvania history prior to the publication, by the Pennsylvania-German Society, of the Narrative and Critical History, under the title : *Pennsylvania: The German Influence in its Settlement and Development.* Its very existence was almost unknown, and still more that of its author, and is now for the first time fully brought to the notice of the public.

How different is the case with the English version of Gabriel Thomas' "Account." The importance of the work has always been more or less recognized, essays have been written upon it ; quotations and extracts printed, and the work itself reprinted in both modern type and facsimile so far back as 1848, and even at the time of writing a fac-simile copy, with annotations, is in course of publication in one of our Western States.

Yet the works of Pastorius and Falckner, which exercised a much greater effect in inducing the emigration of desirable settlers, have thus far, with a single exception, failed to find a champion to suggest a reprint or a fac-simile reproduction of these valuable works.

Geographisch-statistische

Beschreibung

der Provinz

Pensylvanien,

von

Fr. Dan. Pastorius.

Im Auszug mit Anmerkungen.

Memmingen,

bey Andreas Seyler,

1792.

PASTORIUS' BESCHREIBUNG.

Franz Daniel Pastorius'
Beschreibung von Pennsylvanien.

Nachbildung
der in Frankfurt a./M. im Jahre 1700 erschienenen
Original-Ausgabe.

Herausgegeben

vom

Crefelder Verein für wissenschaftliche Vorträge.

Mit einer Einleitung

von

Friedrich Kapp.

Crefeld.
Druck von Kramer & Baum.
1884.

PASTORIUS' BESCHREIBUNG.
FACSIMILE TITLE OF CREFELDER REPRINT OF 1884.

It is true that Pastorius and his works in America did find an able champion in our late lamented Dr. Oswald Seidensticker who, it may be said, was the first to properly introduce Francis Daniel Pastorius to the American public and tell his story of Germantown without, however, bringing about any reissue of his books. The only instance when any such attempt was made was that of the late Friedrich Kapp of Germany who, inspired by the accounts of the bi-centennial celebration, in different parts of the United States, October 6, 1883, of the landing of the Crefelders in Pennsylvania, induced the *Crefelder Verein für Wissenschaftliche Vorträge* in Germany to republish Pastorius' "*Beschreibung*" of 1700. To this Kapp added an introduction, which was mostly a reprint of Seidensticker's *Erste Deutsche Einwanderung.*

The addition, however, was a small one and the book cheaply gotten up. It is now out of print and almost unknown.

Far more important for furthering German emigration than either the works of Pastorius or Thomas, was Falckner's *Curieuse Nachricht,* which gave more authentic information than any of his contemporaries as to the state of the province, the social and domestic affairs of the settlers, and the habits of the Indians, of which Governor Pennypacker, in his "Settlement of Germantown," says: "I know of no other such graphic description."

The combining of the three works in a single volume was a wise provision of the Frankfort Company and shows the acumen of the leading spirits of that organization.

There were other books printed both in German and English during the same decade, advertising the province. A full list of these, together with fac-similes of title-pages and descriptions of each, can be found in my *Father-*

land, in the seventh volume of the Proceedings of the Pennsylvania-German Society.

In the following pages the whole of the original manuscript of Daniel Falckner's *Curieuse Nachricht* will be given both in the original German and a translation, with annotations by the writer. Where the printed version differs from the original manuscript both versions will be given, thus enabling the reader to make his own comparison and deductions.

CHAPTER V.

DANIEL FALCKNER.

DANIEL FALCKNER, author of our *Curieuse Nachricht*, Citizen and Pilgrim in Pennsylvania, in Northern America, as he signs himself therein, was born November 25, 1666, was the second son of Rev. Daniel Falckner, the Lutheran pastor at Langen-Reinsdorf (formerly known as Langen-Rhensdorf and Langeramsdorf), near Crimmitschau, parish of Zwickan, situated in that part of Saxony formerly known as the Markgravate of Meissen, and was a scion of an old Lutheran family. His ancestors on both sides had been ordained Lutheran ministers.

His grandfather, Christian Falckner (died November 5, 1658), as well as his son, Daniel Falckner (died April 7, 1674), father of the subject of our sketch, were both pastors of Langen-Reinsdorf. Pastor Daniel Falckner, the

elder, was a man well versed in many branches of learning besides theology, as his library, an extensive one, contained works upon almost every branch of the arts, sciences, philosophy and history, besides the theological works of the day. This great collection was kept intact until the year 1704, when it was sold at auction. A printed catalogue of this library, which forms a book in itself, is

Daniel Falckner

still preserved in the great *Stadt Bibliothek* of Bremen, and was examined by the writer during the past summer.

Thus it will be seen that the children of Dominie Falckner had exceptional facilities for obtaining knowledge at that early day.

From data that have come down to us, we learn that the subject of our sketch, during his early life, was not of a robust nature, as he was a weak and sickly child from the time of his birth, a condition which changed but little until he came to Pennsylvania, where he himself credits the improvement in his physical condition to the out-door life and exercise in the New World. It will be further noted that in the very introduction to his *Curieuse Nachricht* he makes mention of his " bodily ailments."

The connection of Daniel Falckner with the German Pietists dates from almost the very commencement of the movement which opposed the rigid and externalized orthodoxy in the Lutheran churches in Germany during the close of the Seventeenth Century.

From the correspondence between Spener and Francke, still preserved in the archives of the Halle Orphanage, it

PHILIPP JAKOB SPENER.

B. JAN. 11, 1635; D. FEB. 5, 1705.

appears that Daniel Falckner, the same as both Spener and
Francke, was imbued at the very outset with a belief in the
visions and supernatural powers of several ecstatic maidens,
such as Rosamunda von Asseburg, Anna Maria Schuckart
alias the Erfurth Prophetess and Magdalena Elrichs.
Further that even Daniel Falckner himself at times went
into a state of ecstasy seeing visions and making enraptured
exhortations. A condition from which he was awakened
by the austere Köster. This fact is commented upon by
Spener in a letter to Francke, dated Berlin, May 6, 1693,
some months before the Kelpius party sailed for Pennsylvania, wherein it says : " Thus has Henry Köster brought
Herr Falckner so far that he now has no further *ecstasis*.
He has also told how he came thereto, and how he himself
could by intense imagination awaken divine matters. And
that as he now intends differently and seeks a better path,
he is more calm."

It was not until nine months after this letter was written
by Spener that the long cherished plan of founding a
colony of German Pietists in Pennsylvania was consum-
mated, and the start was made by the party of religious
enthusiasts from Germany to Pennsylvania by way of
England.

Many had been the difficulties in bringing this cherished
object to a final stage of success. Even at the last moment,
when all were ready to embark, Magister Zimmerman
died. This, however, did not deter the party, who continued the voyage under the leadership of Magisters
Kelpius, Köster and Falckner.

There is one important fact in our history that has thus
far failed to attract proper attention. This is nothing more
nor less than the interest the great Spener took in the
success of the German settlement of Pennsylvania. From

letters and memoranda which have come down to us it
appears that Spener and Pastorius were in close touch
during the early days of the latter's residence in Germantown, and that Spener kept himself well informed as to
the state of the Germans in Pennsylvania. That this intercourse ceased upon Pastorius' joining the Quaker fold becomes apparent from Spener's letter of August 1, 1689, viz. :
"I do not remember having heard anything of Herr
Lic. Pastorius since I am here. But would be much
pleased if one of his pamphlets should come to my notice.[5]
Such as take their refuge thither, I leave to their own opinions. I could not advise anyone to flee, before the Lord
drives us out. Thus it appears that yonder place is as
liable to come into danger, as any other. As it stands, the
present English disturbances may also cause some changes
there.

"About Herr Penn it has already been reported for some
time among his own people, that he is not by far what he
formerly was.

" My thoughts are to remain at all times where the Lord
places us, and to remain there so long as he permits, and
to go whenever he commands us to go. Upon such paths
I am surely safe."[6]

Magister Kelpius writes in his Diary that on Monday,
the seventh day of January, 1694, He, being convinced by
God, resolved upon going to America, his companions being
Heinrich Bernhard Köster, Daniel Falckner, Daniel Lutke,

---

[5] Pastorius' Latin missive to Modelius of December, 1688, is evidently indicated here ; so far as known this was not published until April, 1691.

[6] Philipp Jacob Speners, D. Theologische Bedencken, und andere Brief-
fliche Antworten auff geistliche, sondern zur erbauung gerichtete materien zu
unterschiedenen zeiten auffgesetzt, und auff canguirthriges anhalten Christliche freunde in einige ordnung gebracht und herausgegeben. Dritter Theil
Halle, in Verlegung des Waysen-hauses, 1702. From copy in Ev. Luth. Semi-
nary, Mt. Airy, Philadelphia.

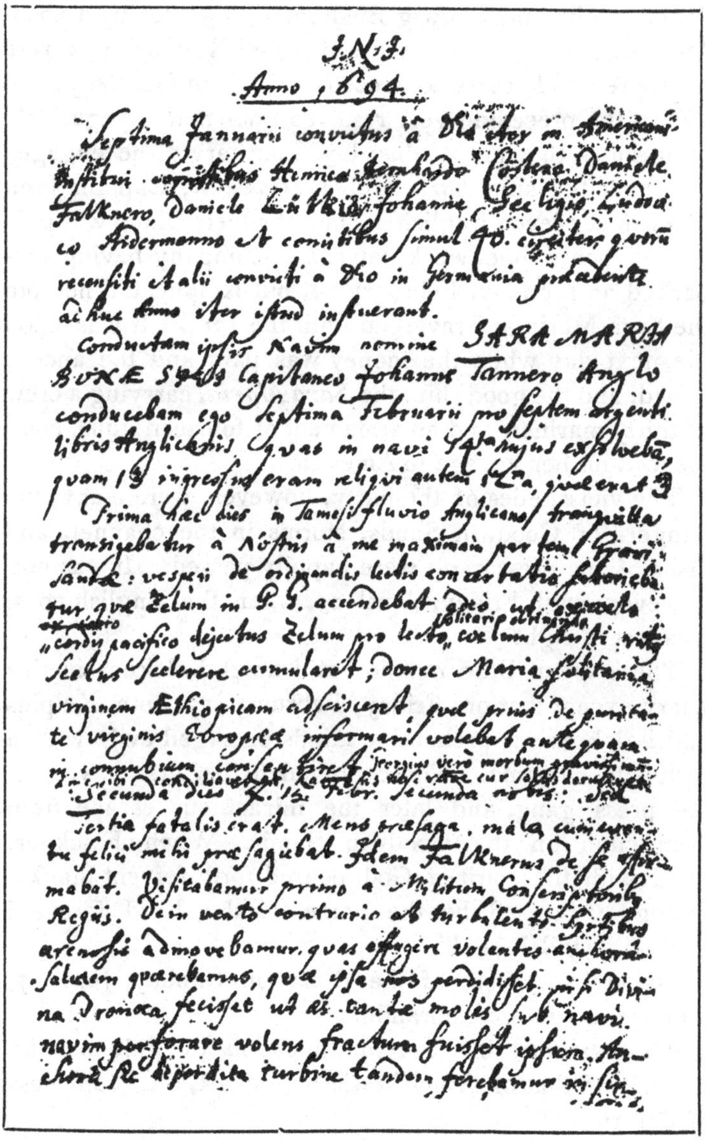
J.N.J.
Anno 1694.

FACSIMILE OF FIRST PAGE OF MAGISTER KELPIUS' DIARY.

Johan Seelig and Ludwig Biederman, together with about
forty other companions, some of whom Kelpius says were
numbered and others convinced by God, in Germany, and
had in the preceding year resolved upon that voyage. He
then states that on Wednesday, February 7, he engaged
for them the ship *Sara Maria Hopewell*, Captain John
Tanner, for seven English pounds of silver, which was paid
out on board one week later, the company having em-
barked on Monday, February 12, but Kelpius did not join
the Sara Maria at Gravesend until the 13th. It was upon
the next day when the money was paid and the anchor
raised, and the good ship, the *Sara Maria*, carrying a crew
of thirty mariners and an armament of fourteen guns, com-
menced on her voyage to America.

The vicissitudes of the party, however, were many, the
dangers of Goodwin Sands, storms in the channel, and
visits of the press gang were happily passed. It was not,
however, until Friday, April 15, when the English coast
was lost to sight.

There is but little mention of Daniel Falckner in this
Diary except that on Friday, February 15, both Kelpius
and Falckner's apprehensive minds presaged evils with a
fortunate outcome. These proved to be, first, a visit of
the press gang, and later the miraculous escape from
destruction on the Goodwin Sands. When Falckner,
filled with the spirit of God, poured forth fervent thanksgiving: "Praised be the name of the Lord forever!
Amen! Hallelujah!"

Toward the close of the Diary on Sunday, June 17,
Kelpius enters a memorandum:

"The memorable excommunication of Falckner by
Köster and that of Anna Maria Schuckart, the Prophetess
of Erfurth."

PORTRAIT OF JOHANNES KELPIUS,
BY CHRISTOPHER WITT IN 1705,
BELIEVED TO BE THE EARLIEST AMERICAN PORTRAIT IN OIL.

This entry in the Kelpius Diary has always been a conundrum to students of Pennsylvania-German history, and has led some to suppose that the woman was among the passengers on the ship.

How Daniel Falckner came to Pennsylvania with this party headed by Magister Kelpius in 1694 and settled on the Wissahickon, has been fully told in my volume on the *German Pietists in Provincial Pennsylvania*, and need not be repeated here. Suffice it to say, as before stated, that late in 1698 or early in 1699 he was sent as an emissary from the Pietists on the Wissahickon to the Fatherland, to make known the true state and spiritual condition of the Germans who had emigrated to Pennsylvania; and to set forth the labors of the Pietistical brethren among their countrymen in America, and solicit aid and additional recruits, so that the perfect number of forty could be kept intact, and at the same time could extend their usefulness in educating their neglected countrymen in Pennsylvania and Virginia.[7]

Another important scheme then under consideration was the emigration of the members of the Philadelphian Society in a body from England and the Continent to settle in Pennsylvania, and there found a colony or colonies where their peculiar teachings should be their only law. And it may easily be inferred that the plan fully outlined in his manuscript and touched upon in the printed version for a Communal Settlement in Pennsylvania upon a cash

---

[7] As a matter of fact there were German settlements in Virginia prior to the beginning of the XVIII. century, as both Köster and Petrus Schäffer journeyed there about the time when Daniel Falckner sailed for Europe. This interesting fact is proven by a manuscript report in the Halle archives from Rev. Pet. rus Schäffer to Rev. August Herman Francke. He also states that he sent a complete history of Virginia to Halle (1699) and requests that it be published. Thus far this interesting manuscript has not been found in the Halle archives.

J. F. S.

capital of 4000 Rix Dollars alludes to the above scheme, if it does not virtually give us some insight into the plan upon which the original settlement of Kelpius and his associates on the Wissahickon was organized.

It is unnecessary here to follow the course of emissary Falckner while upon his visit to the Fatherland: how he reported to Benjamin Furly the Rotterdam merchant, who did so much to promote German emigration, and was subsequently, together with his younger brother, Justus, made attorney in fact, for Furly's holdings in America; or how the Frankfort Company dismissed Pastorius and substituted Falckner, Kelpius and Jawart as attorneys to take charge of and protect their interests in Pennsylvania. All these facts are matters of history and have been fully told in previous publications.

For our present purpose we shall confine ourselves to the chief result of his visit to Halle on the Saale, which was then the great center of German Pietism and religious thought, with Francke as its leader.

AUGUST HERMAN FRANCKE.

B. LUBECK, MAR. 12, 1663; D. HALLE, JUNE 8, 1727.

CHAPTER VI.

August Hermann Francke.

AUGUST HERMANN FRANCKE not only concerned himself with the evangelization or religious condition of Germany, but of America and the East Indies as well. This is attested by the voluminous correspondence with Cotton Mather in New England; Falckner in Pennsylvania; Schäfer in Virginia; Bartlet in Rhode Island, and many others in various places, much of which is still preserved in the archives of the Glaucha Institution.

Accordingly, when Daniel Falckner arrived in Halle, he was cordially received by the elder Francke, and installed at the newly opened orphanage at Glaucha, then a

suburb of Halle. The emissary from Pennsylvania was
requested to render an account of his stewardship, the results obtained by the Pietistical community on the Wissahickon, and finally as before stated to give accurate information of the affairs, both civil and religious, in far-off
Pennsylvania, with special reference to such as might become inclined to transport themselves hither.

For this purpose Francke presented the questions in
writing to Falckner which were intended to cover the
whole field. These interrogations and the answers by
Daniel Falckner cover no less than one hundred and
ninety-seven folio pages.

It is these documents, to which attention is now called,
together with the printed version, which proved so important a factor in guiding the great stream of German emigration to Penn's province on the Delaware.

Daniel Falckner, although one of the prominent charac-
ters during the second decade of Germantown's existence,
little was known of his career to students and historians
in this country, as a scholar, pietist, landagent, bailiff,
attorney and pastor, until some ten or twelve years ago,
when the present Governor of Pennsylvania was compiling
the work known as *The Pennsylvania Colonial cases.*
Wherein for the first time appeared in print Pastorius'
biased account of his difficulties with John Henry Sprögel
and incidentally with Daniel Falckner, thus bringing this

learned pioneer and pietist into public notice after a lapse
of two centuries. Unfortunately in this as in other manuscripts, Pastorius places his successor in office as bailiff
and attorney for the Frankfort Land Company in anything
but a favorable light. Pastorius, himself says that this
was written in 1713 while he was confined to his bed
with a serious illness. It will be noted that this account
(*exemplum sine exemplo*) was written from five to six years
after Daniel Falckner had left the province and taken
charge of several German Evangelical Lutheran Congregations on the Mühlstein and Raritan, in East New Jersey.
Then again as this manuscript, which Pastorius evidently
intended to print, was never made public by him as he
may have been deterred by the fear of legal prosecu-
tion; the accused party had no means of making any
defense against the secret defamation. Thus the matter
remained hidden during all this lapse of years, and when
finally brought to light in Pennypacker's Colonial cases, it
pictured this German pietist and scholar, before the legal
world, in anything but a favorable light, " as such a
spendthrift and ever-drunk, ever-dry, that he made bone
fires of the companies flax in the open street at German
town, giving a bit of silver money to one lad for lighting
his tobacco pipe, and a piece of eight to another for showing him a house in Philadelphia, which in his sober fits he
knew as well as his own."

Under this dark cloud the memory of Daniel Falckner
was obscured until the writer in gathering material for the
publication of his *German Pietists* and investigating the
story of the German mystics, who settled on the banks of
the romantic Wissahickon in the year 1694, found material
which threw an entirely different light upon the life and
character of Daniel Falckner, the writer of the *Curieuse*

Nachricht von Pennsylvanien, a work which proved one of the most effective means to induce German emigration to Pennsylvania.

Further a careful perusal of the preface of Falckner's answers to Francke's interrogations as found among the manuscripts in the archives at Halle, and now for the first time reproduced and translated, will give the best insight into Daniel Falckner's moral and religious bent, while his answers to both manuscript and printed versions will show the careful student, observer and scientist.

In fact, all of the documentary evidence we now have of this early pioneer goes to refute the slanders heaped upon him by the so-called founder of Germantown.

Another point in favor of our claim for this German pietist is that notwithstanding the slanders and defamations heaped upon him by Pastorius, a large tract of land some distance above Germantown, peopled by German settlers, was at that very period named after this same defamed pioneer, and more than that, the church within this tract, of which he undoubtedly was the founder, the oldest German Lutheran congregation in America, even down to the present day, after the lapse of two hundred years is known as the Falckner Swamp Ev. Lutheran Church, a far greater monument to his honor and worth than any granite shaft or brazen tablet.

In bringing this matter again before the public after the lapse of two centuries, the following course has been decided upon. As there is some difference between the original manuscript and the printed version, both versions will be used in the present edition. The published version of 1702 will be printed in heavy German type, any variations or omissions from the original manuscript being inserted in brackets and printed in Roman type. The Ger-

man version will appear upon the left hand pages, with my translation opposite, so far as possible upon corresponding lines. Variations as to numerical arrangement between manuscript and printed version are carefully noted, the whole being amplified by explanatory notes by the translator.

Thus the student, historian and investigator of the future can judge impartially and satisfy himself of both meaning and intent of the pious emissary who compiled this information, as well as the correctness of the translation now presented, which in every case adheres to the original manuscript in preference to the printed version, with the chief aim in view of reproducing as nearly as possible the meaning, phraseology and idiom of the original.

It is a matter of congratulation that this reprint is issued under the auspices of the Pennsylvania-German Society, an organization composed exclusively of descendants of the early German emigrants who came to Pennsylvania during the seventeenth and eighteenth centuries. Many of whose ancestors were led by this very book to forsake the Fatherland with its tyrannies and oppression, and come to the sylvan groves of Penn's Province, build up their homes and erect the altars of their faith and enjoy the personal and religious liberty of the great Quaker experiment, and at the same time become powerful factors in the formation of the grand old Commonwealth of Pennsylvania.

Julius F. Sachse

PHILADELPHIA, October 6, 1903, being the two hundred and twentieth anniversary of the landing of the Crefeldt pioneers.

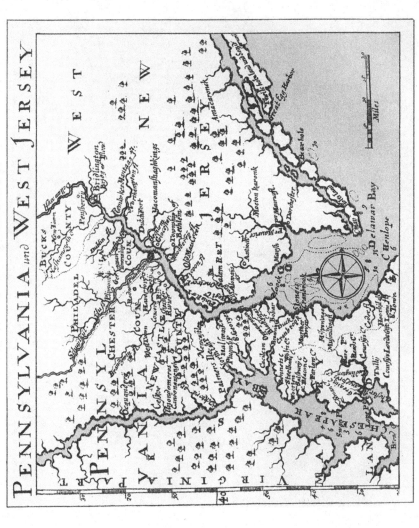

PENNSYLVANIA und WEST JERSEY

MAP FROM EDITION OF 1704.

Curieuſe Nachricht

Von

PENSYLVANIA

in

Norden = America

Welche /

Auf Begehren guter Freunde/

Über vorgelegte 103. Fra=

gen / bey ſeiner Abreiß aus Teutſch=
land nach obigem Lande Anno 1700.
ertheilet/ und nun Anno 1702 in den Druck
gegeben worden.

Von

Daniel Falckner/ Profeſſore,

Burgern und Pilgrim allda.

Franckfurt und Leipzig /
Zu finden bey Andreas Otto/ Buchhändlern,
Im Jahr Chriſti 1702.

THE SEVENTY-THREE ORIGINAL QUESTIONS, TOGETHER
WITH THE TWENTY-TWO ADDITIONAL ONES, PRO-
POUNDED BY REV. AUGUST HERMANN FRANCKE TO
DANIEL FALCKNER UPON HIS RETURN FROM PENNSYL-
VANIA TO GERMANY IN THE YEAR 1699 — AS THEY
APPEAR IN THE HALLE MANUSCRIPT.[1]

(1)   I. Wie die Reise nach America anzustellen?

(2)   II. Wie man sich auf der Reise zu verhalten?

(3)   III. Wie man sich die Reise recht zu nutz zu machen?

(4)   IV. Wie man in specie auf der Reise sich zu seinem
vorhabenden Zweck in America recht *præpariren* könne?

(5)   V. Wofür man sich auf der Reise zu hüten?

(6)   VI. Waß auf dem Schiffe wegen umgang mit den
Schiffleuten in acht zu nehmen?

(7)   VII. Wäßwegen der Schiff= oder See=Krankheit in
acht zu nehmen?

(8) VIII. Wie junge Leute, die einmahl dahin sollen zu
bewußtem Zweck, auf alle Weise dazu zu
præpariren seyn?

(9)   IX. Was bey der Ankunft in Pennsylvania oder
Virginien zu *observiren*?

THE SEVENTY-THREE ORIGINAL QUESTIONS, TOGETHER
WITH THE TWENTY-TWO ADDITIONAL ONES, PRO-
POUNDED BY REV. AUGUST HERMANN FRANCKE TO
DANIEL FALCKNER UPON HIS RETURN FROM PENNSYL-
VANIA TO GERMANY IN THE YEAR 1699 — AS THEY
APPEAR IN THE HALLE MANUSCRIPT.[1]

(1)   I. How to contrive for a voyage to America.

(2)   II. How to conduct oneself upon the voyage.

(3)   III. How one may rightly turn the voyage to profit.

(4)   IV. How one may rightly prepare himself during the voyage for his intended purpose in America.

(5)   V. What one has to beware of on the voyage.

(6)   VI. What one has to be mindful of in his intercourse with the sailors and crew.

(7)   VII. What is to be observed concerning ship or seasickness.

(8)   VIII. How young persons, who intend going there for any specific purpose, are to be properly prepared.

(9)   IX. What is to be observed upon the arrival in Pennsylvania or Virginia.

---

[1] The bracketed numerals refer to corresponding questions in the printed version.

(10)   x. How to conduct oneself there circumspectly and inoffensively toward the divers sects.

(11)   xi. How best to establish oneself, and concerning information about domestic affairs and the household.

(12)   xii. What is to be observed regarding one's health.

(13)   xiii. How the climate is constituted there in summer and winter.

(14)   xiv. Regarding the fertility of the country.

(15)   xv. Of the sorts of fruits and vegetables the country produces.

(16)   xvi. How the Europeans support themselves, and the various ways in which they earn their livelihood.

(17)   xvii. Of the savages, their nations, numbers and languages.

(18)   xviii. How to establish intercourse with them.

(19)   xix. What are their virtues and vices?

(20)   xx. How they live, and what distance their cabins are apart.

(21)   xxi. How they support themselves.

(22)   xxii. How men, women and children spend the day.

(23)   xxiii. How they rear their children.

(24)   xxiv. How do they marry, with what ceremonies, and whether they are polygamous.

(25)   xxv. Do they reward the good and punish the evil, and how?

(27)   xxvi. Of their government. Have they one or many kings; have they any other magistrates, and the king any ministers, or do they rule absolutely alone?

(29)   XXVIII. Wie denen Wilden einige Künste und Wissen=
schafft beyzubringen?

(30)   XXIX. Wie ihnen etwa einige *principia generalia
religionis* bey zu bringen?

(31)   XXX. Wie man ihnen *realiter* das rechtschaffene
Wesen eines Christen vor Augen stellen
könne, daß ihnen das Licht in die Augen
leuchte, und einige Juncken in ihrem Ge=
müthe erwecke?

(32)   XXXI. Wie man meyne das die Wilden in *Americam*
kommen und zwar die unterschiedenen *nationes?*

(33)   XXXII. Wie den Wilden die Teutsche oder Englische
Sprache bey zu bringen?

(34)   XXXIII. Ob nicht bey ihren Kindern solches angehe?

(35)   XXXIV. Ob nicht fromme Teutsche dort ihre Kinder
mit Freundlichkeit an sich halten, und derge=
stalt zur Sprache anleiten können.

(36)   XXXV. Und ob ihnen nicht auf solche Weise gute *principia timoris Dei* bey zu bringen; darauf
noch ferner nach und nach gutes zu erbauen?

(37)   XXXVI. Ob nicht auf diese Weise durch die Kinder
auch die Eltern zu gewinnen?

(38)   XXXVII. Wie die Wilden jetzt ihren *cultum* halten,
was sie anbeten, ob und wie sie opfern?

(39)   XXXVIII. Wie sie vorhin gelebet, ehe die Europäer hin=
ein kamen?

(40)   XXXIX. Was sie nun von den Europäern? angenommen?

(49)   XL. Ob nicht, wenn man fromme Saltzwirker hin=
einschickte, die Saltzquellen bey Philadel=
phia mit großem Vortheil zu gebrauchen,
und durch solche dann das Gute dort beför=
dert werden könte?

(28) XXVII. Wherein the king differs from the others in dress, habitation, outward authority, etc.

(29) XXVIII. How to introduce some of the arts and sciences among the savages.

(30) XXIX. How to introduce among them some of the general principles of religion.

(31) XXX. How one could properly place before them the true righteous nature of a Christian, so that the light would shine into their eyes, and divers sparks awaken their nature.

(32) XXXI. How it is supposed that the savages came to America, and in particular the different nations.

(33) XXXII. How to introduce the German or English tongue among the savages.

(34) XXXIII. Would such be possible with their children?

(35) XXXIV. Whether devout Germans there could not by friendliness attach their children unto them, and in such manner induce them to learn the language.

(36) XXXV. Whether in this manner good *principia timoris Dei* might not be impressed upon them, whereupon to gradually build good results.

(37) XXXVI. Could we not in this manner reach the elders through the children?

(38) XXXVII. How the savages now keep their cult, what they worship, and as to their sacrificial rite.

(39) XXXVIII. How they lived prior to the advent of the Europeans.

(40) XXXIX. What they have adopted from the Europeans.

(50) XLI. So auch mit fromme Berg=Leuten?

(51) XLII. Eine *geographische* Beschreibung von *Pensylvania, Virginia* und ander nahe gelegen Ländern und Insuln.

(52) XLIII. Wie es mit der *Correspondence* in *Americam* und wieder heraus zu halten?

(53) XLIV. Ob nicht allerhand Handwercker drinnen können fortkommen oder welche fürnehmlich?

(54) XLV. Wie man gute erbauliche Schrifften? hinein zu bringen in *Teutscher, Englischer, Schwedischer, Frantzösischer* Sprache, die *nationes* so in *Pensylvania, Virginia, neu- Engelland* seyn, dadurch kräfftig zu erbauen?

(55) XLVI. Wie man Leute recht *philadelphischen* Geistes von *Schweden, Engelländern, Deutschen* und von allen *religionen,* so darinnen sind zu suchen, die zur Forderung des Werckes des Herrn einander die Hand recht bieten könten?

(56) XLVII. Wie alt die Wilden werden?

(57) XLVIII. Ob ihre Weiber einander in der Geburth beystehen?

(58) XLIX. Wie sie es mit den gantz kleinen Kindern halten?

(59) L. Was für Flüsse da seyn?

(60) LI. Wie sie gebrauchet werden?

(61) LII. Wie sie ihre Fischereyen halten?

(62) LIII. Und ihre Jagen?

(63) LIV. Was für Thiere da seyen, Zahme und Wilde?

(64) LV. Was für Vögel?

(65) LVI. Wie man sich gegen die Bären und andere wilde Thiere bewahre?

(49)   XL. If pious salt workers were sent over to develop the saline springs near Philadelphia, could they not be used with great profit, and through them further that which is good?

(50)   XLI. How about pious miners?

(51)   XLII. A geographical description of Pennsylvania and adjacent countries and islands.

(52)   XLIII. How about correspondence with America, and from thence outward?

(53)   XLIV. Whether all kinds of artisans cannot find subsistence there, and which in particular.

(54)   XLV. How to introduce good devout literature in the English and French languages for an energetic edification of such nationalities as have settled in Pennsylvania, Virginia and New England.

(55)   XLVI. How to seek out persons imbued with a true Philadelphian spirit from among the Swedes, English and all religious persuasions who are there, and would be willing to extend their hands to one another in the furtherance of the word of the Lord.

(56)   XLVII. To what age do the savages attain?

(57)   XLVIII. Do the women assist each other during parturition?

(58)   XLIX. How do they care for their infants?

(59)   L. What rivers are there?

(60)   LI. How are they utilized?

(61)   LII. How is fishing followed?

(62)   LIII. Concerning their hunting.

(63)   LIV. What kinds of animals are there, both domestic and wild?

(66)   LVII. Womit die Wilden bishero ſonderlich von den
                    Europeern geärgert, und zum Theil noch
                    ſchlimmer gemacht werden?

            LVIII. Wie ſolch Aergerniß zu *emendiren?*

(67)   LIX. Wie man lauter nutzliche Künſte und Wiſſen=
                    ſchafften in *Americam* bringen könne? Die
                    Böſen, unnützen und unnöthigen weg laſſen.

(68)   LX. Wie das Land zu ſeinem rechten Gebrauch und
                    Nutzen zu bringen?

(69)   LXI. Wenn chriſtliche Leute hinein wollen, die grobe
                    äuſſerliche Arbeit nicht verrichten können,
                    wie man ſie zu gebrauchen wiſſe und wie ſie
                    ſich nähren können, ob durch *information*
                    oder noch auf andere Weiſe?

(70)   LXII. Wenn neue *Colonien* hinein kommen, ob ſie
                    ſich zu den alten ſchlagen müſſen, oder ob ſie
                    ſelbſt eine neue Stadt anrichten können?

(71)   LXIII. Was für Vorſchläge zu einer ſolchen neuen
                    Colonie zu thun ſeyn?

(72)   LXIV. Wie in *specie* es damit einzurichten, das die
                    Nachkommen ſich einer guten Ordnung in
                    allen Stücken möchten zu erfreuen haben?

(73)   LXV. In was für Ordnung die Itzigen *Colonien*
                    ſtehen, wie ſie vom *Magistrat* regiert wer=
                    den, wie dem böſen gewehret, wie das gute
                    befördert wird?

(74)   LXVI. Was man gutes und rechtſchaffenes darunter
                    finde?

(75)   LXVII. Wie die Städte in Penſylvania alle heißen,
                    wie weit ſie von einander gelegen, wie ſie
                    gelegen, an was vor Flüſſen, was ſie für
                    Gemächlichkeit haben, wie viel Häuſer und
                    Einwohner? Ob in einer jeden Stadt

(64)   LV. What kinds of birds are there?

(65)   LVI. How to protect oneself against bears and other wild beasts.

(66)   LVII. Whereby the savages have thus far been irritated by the Europeans, and are partly made still worse.

    LVIII. How such irritation may be amended.

(67)   LIX. How to introduce purely advantageous arts and sciences into America, and eliminate the evil and useless ones.

(68)   LX. How to develop the country and bring about its proper uses and advantages.

(69)   LXI. If Christian people want to come in, who could not perform the ordinary rough work, how could they be made useful, and sustain themselves? If through information or otherwise.

(70)   LXII. When new colonies come over, must they join one of the older ones, or must they build a new town for themselves?

(71)   LXIII. What suggestions are to be made to such a new colony?

(72)   LXIV. How in particular to make arrangements, so that those who follow may enjoy good order in every way.

(73)   LXV. Under what regulations do the present colonies stand, and how are they governed by the magistrates? How is evil combated, and the good encouraged?

(74)   LXVI. What is to be found amongst them, that is good and righteous?

(75)   LXVII. How are all the towns in Pennsylvania named, and how far are they apart, upon

unterschiedliche *Secten* oder *religionen*, oder in einiger nur eine?

(76) LXVIII. Wohin und auf was Weise, und womit der Handel in Pensylvania getrieben wird?

(77) LXIX. Auf was Weise man sich dessen zu einem Vortheil in Erweiterung des Reiches Gottes bedienen könne?

(78) LXX. Und wenn dadurch dem Reiche Gottes einiger Schaden geschiehet ob nicht solchem auf einige Weise zu begegnen?

(79) LXXI. Was von *particulier Historien* bekannt ist, so sich mit den Wilden zu getragen.

[1]Desgleichen *Historien* unter denen *nationen* selbst so in *Americam* kommen, so einige gute Erinnerung oder Nachricht etwa an die Hand geben könte?

(80) LXXII. Was von dem Zustande anderer Länder oder *Insulen* in *America* bekant ist, *inprimis quoad statum religionis Christianæ?*

(81) Wie in *Pennsylvania* mit einigem Capital ein *Profit* zu machen?

---

[1] This question is LXXII in the original list of questions. No reply, however, appears to have been made to it, as the next question (80) appears as LXXII.

what rivers and their conveniences, the
number of houses and inhabitants, and if
in every town there are divers sects and
religions, or only one?

(76) LXVIII. The commerce of Pennsylvania, whereto, in
what manner, and wherein does it consist?

(77) LXIX. In what manner could this be made to serve
to the advantage and extension of the
kingdom of God?

(78) LXX. Should anything arise thereby prejudicial
to the kingdom of God, could it not be
overcome in some manner?

(79) LXXI. What particular histories are known concerning the savages?

LXXII. Likewise traditions current among the settlers themselves who have come to America, which would give some good remin-
iscences or accounts thereof.

(80) LXXIII. What is known about the condition of the
other countries and islands in America:
*Imprimis quoad statum religionis Chris-
tianæ?*

(81) LXXIV. How to make profit with capital in Pennsylvania.

ADDITAMENTUM QUÆSTIONUM.

(82) LXXIII. Woran in America Mangel sey?

(83) LXXIV. Woher man ein jedes nothwendiges Ding bekommen kan?

(84) LXXV. Was die Europäer aus Engelland und Holland von dergleichen Dingen vornehmlich mit zu nehmen haben?

(85) LXXVI. Was man sonderlich aus Holland oder Engelland zur Leibes und Gesundheit Pflege mit zu Schiffe zu nehmen habe?

(86) LXXVII. Bey wem man sich bey seiner Ankunft in America am ersten zu melden habe?

(87) LXXVIII. Ob auch einem Europäer frey stehe, mit seinem in America erworbenen Gute wieder nach seinem Belieben zurück zu kehren?

(88) LXXIX. An was für Handwerksleuten es daselbst am meisten fehle?

(89) LXXX. Wie es die Wilden bey dem Begräbniß ihrer Todten halten?

(90) LXXXI. Ob der Eidschwur bey ihnen Bräuchlich, wie solches geschehe und bey wem sie schwören?

(91) LXXXII. Ob die Wilden den siebenden Tag heiligen und wie sie solchen feyern?

(92) LXXXIII. Ob bei den Wilden nicht einiges Verlangen nach dem wahren Erkänntniß Gottes zu finden wenn diejenigen so ihre Sprache verstehen, mit ihnen reden?

(93) LXXXIV. Was die Wilden von der Auferstehung der Todten halten und glauben?

ADDITAMENTUM QUÆSTIONUM.

(82)   LXXIII. Whereof is there a deficiency in America?

(83)   LXXIV. Where are all necessary things to be obtained?

(84)   LXXV. What the Europeans have chiefly to bring with them from England and Holland.

(85)   LXXVI. What should be taken on shipboard from Holland for the special benefit of the body and health.

(86)   LXXVII. To whom must one report firstly upon his arrival in America?

(87) LXXVIII. Is a European at liberty to return at his pleasure, with such property as he has acquired in America?

(88)   LXXIX. What manner of handicraftsmen are mostly wanting?

(89)   LXXX. How do the savages act at the burial of their dead?

(90)   LXXXI. Is an oath customary amongst them, and how is it administered, and by whom?

(91)   LXXXII. Whether the savages sanctify the seventh day, and how they observe it.

(92) LXXXIII. Whether there is evident among the savages some longing after a true knowledge of God, when such as speak their language talk with them.

(93) LXXXIV. What the savages hold and believe of a resurrection of the dead.

(94)   LXXXIV. Was die wilden Leute für Gewehr führen?

(95)   LXXXVI. Ob nicht einige *Philosophi* oder gelehrte
        Leute unter den Wilden, worinn sie sich
        üben und ob sie auch den Lauf des Himmels
        observiren?

(96)   LXXXVII. Ob die Wilden auch einige ausserordentliche
        Zeichen observiren und erkennen?

(97)   LXXXVIII. Ob nicht unter ihnen auch einige *motus* oder
        Bewegungen zu spüren?

(98)   LXXXIX. Ob nicht unter denen Secten auch einige unge=
        wöhnliche bewegungen und vorbothen der
        herannahenden Gerichte Gottes zu spüren?

(99)   XC. Wie sich die sogenannten Geistlichen unter den
        mancherley Secten in America aufführen
        und sowohl unter sich selbst, als gegen andere
        comportiren?

(100) XCI. Was vor Hoffnung sey, daß die mancherley
        Secten in eins zusammen treten möchten?

(101) XCII. Durch was für Mittel man die Wilden am
        meisten an sich ziehe oder wodurch sie am
        meisten abgewendet werden.

(102) XCIII. Was die Wilden für Nahmen führen?

(103) XCIV. Wenn sie ihren Kindern Nahmen geben?

(94) LXXXV. What sort of arms the savages carry?

(95) LXXXVI. Whether there be not some philosophers or learned men amongst the savages; what they practice and whether they observe the course of the heavens?

(96) LXXXVII. Do the savages also observe any extraordinary phenomena and understand them?

(97) LXXXVIII. Do not some among them perceive any *motus* or agitation?

(98) LXXXIX. If there be not some unusual manifestation perceived among the sects of the harbinger of the approaching millennium?

(99) XC. How the so-called ecclesiastics among the manifold sects in America conduct themselves toward each other, and how they comport themselves toward others.

(100) XCI. What hope is there that the divers sects may come together as one?

(101) XCII. By what means can the savages best be drawn toward us, and whereby are they mostly repelled?

(102) XCIII. What manner of names the savages have?

(103) XCIV. When do they name their children?

NINE QUESTIONS IN THE PRINTED VERSION WHICH DO
NOT APPEAR IN THE ORIGINAL MANUSCRIPT PRESERVED
IN THE HALLE ARCHIVES.

(25)   Von der Wilden ihre Sprache und umbgang?

(41)   Von den Wilden ihren Curen und Kranck=
              heiten?

(42)   Was die Wilden für Krieg führen?

(43)   Von der Wilden ihrer eigentlichen Haus=
              halten?

(44)   Von der Wilden ihrem Hausrathe.

(45)   Von denen Thieren, so in *Pensylvania* zu
              befinden.

(46)   Was gibt es dann für Wasser Thiere?

(47)   Was gibt es dann für Schädliche Thier im
              Wasser?

(48)   Was siehet man dann auf denen Wasser=
              flüssen für Thiere schwimmen?

———

[FROM HALLE MANUSCRIPT.]

Wie in *Pennsylvania* mit einigem Capital ein *Profit* zu
machen?

———

Lysta derjenigen Wahren, so in *Pensylvanien* angenehm sind.
Nach H. Falckner seinem Behalt aufgezeichnet.

———

NINE QUESTIONS IN THE PRINTED VERSION WHICH DO
NOT APPEAR IN THE ORIGINAL MANUSCRIPT PRESERVED
IN THE HALLE ARCHIVES.

(25)	Of the savages their speech and inter-course.
(41)	Concerning the diseases and cures of the savages.
(42)	The warfare of the savages.
(43)	Of the domestic life of the savages.
(44)	Of the savage's household utensils.
(45)	Of the animals to be found in Pennsylvania.
(46)	What kind of aquatic animals are there?
(47)	What kind of dangerous animals are in the waters there?
(48)	What animals are to be seen swimming upon the water courses?

[FROM HALLE MANUSCRIPT.]

How to make profit with capital in Pennsylvania.

List of articles, which in the opinion of Herr Falckner would prove acceptable in Pennsylvania.

PRÆMONITIO.

Daß ich diese Fragen nicht *sufficient* beantworten kan, ist die Zeit, die Menge meiner Verrichtungen und die Ungewohnheit sich in äusseren auf so mancherley Art auszubreiten schuld, darzu kommt, daß ich mich der Unpäßlichkeit meines Leibes halber aller Dinge mit eins so nicht erinnern kan, welche ich doch einzeln hin und wieder ausgesaget. Einige Sachen sind, darumb ich mich dieselben *accurat* zu wissen, auch in America nicht bekümmert, deswegen ich dieselben biß auf weiteren Bescheid versparen muß denn ich wollte nicht gerne etwas ungewisses schreiben. Inzwischen wird sich Niemand an meiner Schreibart kehren, welche *stilo seculi expers* ist; sondern aus vielen dasjenige erwehlen, was ihm anstehet, gnug daß ich in allen und bey allen den geneigten Leser versichern kan, daß ich weiß an wen ich glaube und auch gewiß bin, daß derselbige HErr mir meine Beilage bewahren kan, ja will, biß an jenen Tage; deswegen ich auch große Freudigkeit gebrauche, den Todt und allen Verderben trotz zu biethen, weil ich gerne so kühne auf den Fels meines Heils sein wolte, als immer ein Mensch auf seine unüberwindliche Festung. Es ist mir Gottlob gelungen, und ich sehe daß es anderen auch gelinget,

PRÆMONITIO.

[PREFACE TO THE ORIGINAL MANUSCRIPT IN THE
ARCHIVE AT HALLE.]

The reasons why I cannot answer these questions satis-
factorily, is because of a lack of time, and the number of
my engagements, together with being unaccustomed to
express myself publicly upon so many subjects. And on
account of my physical infirmities I fail to remember some
of the things of which I have now and then spoken upon
other occasions. Then there are some things concerning
which I have not troubled myself to learn about in America.
These I must hold in reserve until I shall have further
information, as I do not wish willingly to write about anything that I am not quite sure of. In the meantime let no
one find fault with the style of my composition which is
stilo seculi expers. but let him select from the abundance
thereof that which pleases him. It is enough, that I can
assure the kindly disposed reader, that in all and by all, I
know in whom I have believed, and am persuaded, that the
same Lord can secure my consummation, yea will, even
unto that day: for which reason I also take great pleasure
in hurling defiance at death and all corruption. In as
much as I would place myself as boldly upon the rock of

(65)

die einerley hoffnung mit mir sind. Hallelujah. Ferner wie ich
in einfältiger liebe zu meinen Vaterland und bekanten durch
Gottes willen wiedergekehret bin, als habe ich auch bey meiner
Reise bißhero nichts anderes beobachtet, als das der Leib Christi
erbauet werden mögte. Ich habe zum wenigsten die Liebe zum
Frieden gerathen, was schwach ist gestärket, die Müden ermuntert, den Vorwitz gestrafet, und mich mit denen in Hoffnung
lebenden gefreuet, und gehe nun gestärcket, wiewohl der sinnlichen
Empfindung nach fast müde, wieder hin, ob Gott will *Germaniam*
in America zu sehen und mich daselbst zu bezeugen, wie es mein
König der Könige von mir erfordert, darzu ich mich dem Gebeht
und der Liebe aller wahren glieder des Leibes Jesu empfohlen
haben will. Ich protestire aber hiermit noch mahls christlich,
gleich wie ich dasselbe nach erforderter Gelegenheit mündlich
gethan, daß ich nicht *intendiret*, jemand durch mein kommen oder
weggehen oder Reden zur Versuchung oder Beschwerung zu seyn,
vielweniger jemanden hinaus in die Wüsten zu führen. Es gehe
ein jeglicher zu Christo, dessen die gantze Erde ist und ihre Fülle
und lerne von Ihm, was er thun solle, so kan er auch das Erd-
reich besitzen. Doch habe ich dem lieben Teutschland hin und
wieder etwas altes aufs neue gesaget und sage es allen mit
Lutheri Worten noch einmahl, welche zu finden in der Vermahn-
ung an die Städte in Teutschland; Lieben Deutschen — das solt
ihr wissen, Gottes Wort und Gnade ist ein Fahrender Platzregen,
der nicht wieder kommt, wo er einmahl gewesen, er ist bey den
Juden gewesen, aber hin ist hin, sie haben nun nichts, Paulus
brachte ihn in Griechenland, aber hin ist auch hin, sie haben nun
den Pabst und ihr Teutsche dürft nicht denken, daß ihr ihn ewig
haben werdet, denn der undank und Verachtung wird ihn euch
nicht ewig lassen bleiben. Darumb greifft zu und haltet, wer

my salvation, as ever a man stood upon an impregnable
fortress. Thank God! I have succeeded, and that others
having the same hope will likewise succeed. Hallelujah.

Further as I in artless simplicity have by God's will
returned to my fatherland and acquaintances will say that
during my journey thus far, I have observed nought but
how the body of Christ is being built up. I have at least
always counselled in the interest of charity and Peace,
strengthened that which was weak, encouraged the weary,
corrected the froward and rejoiced with those living in
hope, and now I go quickened in spirit, though in a bodily
sense almost weary, to return, if it please God, to see again
Germanian in America, and testify there as my King of
Kings demands of me. For which I will have to commend
myself to the love and prayers of all true members of the
body of Christ. I, however, again offer here a Christian
protest, just as I have done verbally upon previous occasions, that it is not intended, that I should prove a temptation or burden to any one, that my coming, going and what I
say should induce anyone to go out into the wilderness:
Let every one go unto Christ, to whom belongs the whole
earth, and the fullness thereof, and learn from Him, what to
do, then he too shall possess the earth. Yet I have here
and there told anew to dear old Germany, things that were
old, and now proclaim to all, once again in Luther's words,
which are to be found in his "Admonition to the cities of
Germany": Beloved Germans, this you ought to know,
that, God's word and grace is like unto a sudden driving
thunder storm, which does not again return to where it
once was. It was thus with the Jews, but what is gone is
gone and now they have nothing. Paul brought it into
Greece, but there what is gone is gone, and they now have
the Pope, and you Germans, must not think that you will

halten kan, faule Hände müssen ein böses Jahr haben, item über
den 123 Psalm.

Jetzt wird Gottes Wort der Welt häufig und mit Menge vor=
getragen, man prediget es in den Kirchen, man findet es in denen
Büchern, man pfeiffts uns, man singts uns, man mahlet es an
die Wände, aber was geschicht, der meiste Theil achtet es nicht,
und die Fürsten und Könige verfolgen es aufs jämmerlichste,
schelten und vernichten es.   *Sapienti satis.*

Es hat die Klage seid der Reformation immer gewähret, wie
daß das evangelische Häuslein in Ansehung des Pabstthums und
der Ungläubigen ein so weniges von dem Erdboden inne hat aber
was ist die Schuldt, der Faule sagt Salomon, stirbet über dem
wünschen, inzwischen hat das Pabstthum Hand angeleget, und hat
denselben niemahls an Autoritat und Hülfe ihrer Oberen, an
Mitteln und Menschen gefehlet, ihre lehre in aller Welt auszu=
breiten, auch unter vielen Trübsaalen und leiden; hätten sie nun
die lautere Wahrheit vor sich so wäre ihr Eifer recht göttlich zu
heißen, doch beschämen sie uns in unserer protestantisch evangeli=
schen Kirche, darinnen wir gar nichts thäten, wo wir nicht müssen.
O wie sanft haben unsere Herren bißhero auf den Stiften ge=
ruhet, die das Pabstthum meistentheils vor sie gestiftet, und die
Beute, die Gott bey der Reformation gegeben frühzeitig im
Schweißtuch vergraben.   Daher wird sie Gott auch wieder von
ihren falschen Ruhe=Lagern aufftreiben, zumahl der Menschen im
Unglauben viel geworden und einander trucken ob schon Kriege
und Plagen frißt, was es kann und findet, welches der seelige
Lutherus schon gefürchtet, da er unter andern in Tischreden fol.
598 sagt: „Ich fürchte Teutschland sey verrathen und verkauft,
es wird erschöpft beyde von Geld und Leuten und gar ausgesogen.
Hilft uns Gott nicht so sind wir verloren.   Es kan so nicht blei=
ben, wie es nun ist, und daß es vor das erste besser werden soll,

have it forever,[1] for your ingratitude and contempt will not permit it to remain. Therefore grasp and hold whosoever can, idle hands must have a bad year, likewise see Psalm CXXIII.[2]

At the present time God's word is frequently and abundantly preached to the world, it is proclaimed in the churches, it is found in books, it is piped to us; it is sung to us; it is painted upon the walls. Yet what happens? The majority pay no heed to it, and the kings and nobles persecute it most deplorably, revile and destroy it. *Sapienti satis.*

Since the Reformation the complaint has steadily prevailed, that the little envangelical flock possess so little of this earth, in comparison with the Papacy and unbelievers. Now what is the reason? The sluggard says Solomon, dieth over his own wishes.[3] Meanwhile the Papacy has fastened its hand, and the authority of the superiors, and their assistance with men and means, is never wanting to spread their doctrine throughout the world, even under the greatest tribulations and suffering. Had they but the pure truth before them, then their zeal might be called truly godly. Yet they shame us in our Protestant Evangelical churches, in so far that we do nought but what we are forced to do. Oh! how placid our clergy have thus far rested in the beneficent institutions, which the Papacy had mostly founded before them, and the treasures which God gave them at the time of the Reformation were prematurely buried in the napkin. Therefore the Lord will again arouse them from their false resting place, more especially as mankind has increased so greatly in infidelity and crowd one another, although war and pestilence destroys what it can find and reach. All of which the sainted Luther already feared, when he said among other things in his

sehe ich nicht. Denn es kommt ein ander König und eine andere
Zeit, die weiß von Joseph nichts."

Darum werden nach Danielis Aussage in den letzten Zeiten
viele geläutert und gereinigt werden. Die Gottlosen aber wer=
den es nicht achten. Das künftige Elend wird viele gehen heis=
sen und zur Reise da und dorthin *præpariren*, die sich es vorher
nicht eingebildet. Ich möchte wünschen zu wissen, was viele von
den Pfältzern gedächten, die also unversehens von ihrer Habe und
Plaisir entrissen, an unseren Thüren das Brot betteln, bey derer
Anschauung Teutschland die Güte auch den Ernst Gottes erkennen
möchte. Doch es heißt: *qualis rex, talis grex*, die Fürsten
wollen doch gerne Land haben, und suchen alle stätischen Griffe
und *prætensionen* deshalben hierfür, doch wollen sie dieselben am
liebsten, wo große Festungen sind, wo Silber und Gold ist, wo
Tyro und Sidon auf großen Schiffen aus und ein führet, daß
und wie aber Gottes Wort laufen möge, und wie man den Heyden
auch Gelegenheit gebe, den Nahmen des Herrn zu erkennen (wel=
ches allein ein recht Königlich Werck ist) bekümmert sich niemand
darum, ja Christus selbst muß sich in ihren eigenen Grentzen ja
nicht zu breit machen, so bleiben denn auch die Gemeinen, die ihr
guts feines Auskommen samt dem Ansehen und äusserliches renome
im Christenthum haben, im Lande, und nehren sich, wie sie sagen
redlich: wo bleibt der Arme, welcher von der Schinderey errettet
werden soll? Doch ist der Herr des Armen Schutz. Darumb
fürchte ich abermahl und beschreibe mit Lutheri Worten, was ein
mit unzehligen Wohlthaten von Gott begnadigtes doch undanck=
bahres Volck sich endlich zu versehen hat. „Gedenket doch wie
viel Güter euch euer Gott umsonst gegeben und noch täglich giebt,
nembl. Leib und Seel, Hauß und Hof, Weib und Kind, darzu
weltlichen Frieden, Dienst und Brauch aller Creaturen im Him=
mel und auf Erden über das alles auch das Evangelium und

Tabletalk (folio 598): "I fear that Germany is betrayed and sold, it is being drained of both money and people and indeed impoverished. Unless the Lord help us we are lost. It cannot continue thus, as it is now, but I do not perceive that it will better itself in the near future. For there comes another King and another time, that knows nought of Joseph." Therefore according unto Daniel's testimony in these later times "Many shall be purified, and made white and tried; but none of the wicked shall understand."[4] The coming misery will cause many to go, and prepare for a journey to this place and that, who have not previously contemplated it. I would like to know just what many of the Palatines think, who so unexpectedly had their possessions and pleasures wrested from them, and now beg for bread at our doors. By the contemplation of which, Germany may comprehend the goodness as well as the sternness of God. Though it is said *Qualis Rex— talis grex* (Like Lord, like herd). The princes seek to gain more territory, and seek by all statistical tricks and pretentions to acquire it. They have a preference for such as have large fortifications, where silver and gold abound, where great ships sail to and from Tyre and Sidon. But for God's holy word and how to afford the heathen an opportunity to learn the name of the Lord (which alone is a right royal work) no one has any concern—yea even the Lord Jesus himself must not be too much in evidence within their borders. Thus, there remain the congregations of the land who enjoy their good competency together with the respectability and outward reputation of Christianity, and support themselves as they say honestly. But what becomes of the poor who are to be saved from oppression? However, of these the Lord is the protector. Therefore I am again apprehensive and will set forth in Luther's words

Predigt-Ambt, Taufe und Sacrament und den gantzen Schatz seines Sohnes und seines Geistes nicht allein ohne dein Verdienst, sondern auch ohne deine Kosten und Mühe, aber du willst nicht ein Tröpflein Dankes erzeigen, sondern Gottes Reich und der Seelen Heil lassen untergehen und helfen stoßen. Solte Gott hierüber nicht zornig werden, solte nicht theure Zeit kommen, solt nicht Pestilentz, Schweiß, Frantzosen und andere Plagen uns finden, solten nicht verblendete Leute, wilde wüste Tyrannen regieren, solt nicht Krieg und Hader entstehen, solt nicht ein böses Regiment in teutschen Landen werden, solten nicht Türcken und Tartaren uns plündern; Ja, es wäre nicht wunder, daß Gott beyde Thür und Fenster in der Hölle aufthäte und ließe unter uns lauter Teufel schneien und schlacken und ließ von Himmel regnen Schwefel und höllisch Feuer und versenkte uns allesamt in Abgrund der Höllen wie Sodoma und Gomorra; Denn hätte Sodoma und Gomorra so viel gehabt so viel gehört oder gesehen, sie stünden noch heutigen Tages. Denn sie sind das zehende Theil nicht so böse gewesen als jetzo Teutschland ist.

Denn sie haben Gottes Wort und Predig-Ambt nicht gehabt so haben wir es umbsonst und stellen uns, als die da wollten, daß beyde Gott sein Wort, alle Zucht und Ehre unterginge. Wann es so soll in Teutschland gehen, so ist mirs Leyd, daß ich ein Teutscher gebohren bin, oder je teutsch geredet oder geschrieben habe, und wo ich es für mein Gewissen thun könte, wolte ich wieder dazu rathen und helfen, daß der Pabst mit allen seinen Greueln wieder über uns kommen müßte und ärger trucken, schanden und verderben, denn je zuvor geschehen etc. in der Predigt von der Kinder-Schul. Inzwischen bleibt bey einem rechten Bürger Jerusalems reisen und zu Hause bleiben eine resolution und wird sich niemand an dem närrischen Abraham ärgern, wer dieses verstehet, daß er nirgends bleiben könte in den Tagen der grenlichen

what a people eventually have to perform, who having received numberless blessings and pardon from God, and are yet ungrateful. "Pray remember how many blessings your Lord hath bestowed unto you for nought and still gives you daily, namely: Your body and soul, your home and grounds; your wife and child; together with the universal peace, the service and use of all creatures in the air and upon the earth, but above all the Gospels and ministry, Baptism and the Lord's Supper, and all the treasures of his Son and Spirit, not only without any merit on your part, but even without cost or labor upon your part, yet you will not render a modicum of thanks, but let God's realm and your soul's salvation be wrecked and never help to prosecute it. And ought not the Lord become angry with you? Ought not a time of dearth and famine to come unto you, ought not pestilence, sweating sickness [5] the French and other plagues overtake you? Ought not deluded men, wild dissolute tyrants rule over us? Ought not war and strife arise, should not an evil government come about in the German States, and the Turks and Tartars plunder us? Yea it were no wonder, if God were to open both doors and the windows of Hell, and let loose among us nothing but devils and rain upon us from heaven brimstone and hell fire, and cast us all down into the very bottomless pit of hell, as He did Sodom and Gomorra. For had Sodom and Gomorra possessed, heard and seen as much, they would be still standing at the present day. For they were not one-tenth as wicked as Germany is at present, they had neither God's Holy Word nor the ministry, we have it gratuitously, but place ourselves, among such as would, that the Lord, his word, discipline and honor perish. If this is to be the rule in Germany, I shall regret that I am born a German, or ever spoke or wrote German, and if

Blindheit Iſraelis. Es werde nun hier und da in der Welt, wie es hier und dort iſt, ſo wird es hier doch noch ſchlimmer ſeyn, wann es dort geworden iſt, wie es hier war. Die Welt tröſtet ſich zwar und ihre Kinder, ſagend: O, es iſt alle Zeit ſo böſe geweſen, es war vor dieſem auch ſo, aber von Anfang wars nicht alſo, und wird der zur äußerſten Geduld gewartete Baum endlich die Axt leyden müſſen und zwar von der wurtzel aus. Es darf mir niemand nach America folgen, den wer weiß, wie lange ich da bin, daß ich aber allda bin, weiß ich und die treue Göttliche providenz. Urſachen dafür, welche zu ehren in Lobe und in Freude mein Werck ſeyn wird, ſo lang ich dort und hier bin. Was ſonſt noch zu erinnern wäre, wird aus einigen Sätzen von der *ratione peregrinandi* in gegenwärtiger Zeit zu erſehen ſeyn, deswegen den Gelehrten und Geliebten Leſer der Treue Gottes in Chriſto und dem Worte ſeiner Geduld empfehle und verbleibe mitkämpfend, mitleidend und mithoffend an dem Leibe Jeſu, der über die gantze Erde zerſtreuet, erwartet ſeines Ertzhirten und Königs mit ſehnlichem Verlangen.

Daniel Falckner,
Bürger und Pilgrim von Penſylvanien
in Nordern America.

I could but do it conscientiously, I would advise and even help that the Pope, with all his abominations, might again be over us, and oppress, injure and corrupt us, worse than ever before etc." (in his sermon of the Infant School).

Meanwhile a true citizen of Jerusalem will abide by his resolution either to travel or to stay at home, and no one familiar with the circumstances will blame foolish Abraham for not wishing to stay at any one place in the horrible days of Israel's blindness.

May it now come about here and there in the world, as it is there and yonder, so it will be even worse here, when it comes about yonder, as it was here. The world indeed consoles itself and its children saying : Oh! every age has been as bad as the present, formerly it was even so. But in the beginning it was not always so. And when finally all patience with the tree has been exhausted the axe must be applied to the very root. No one must follow me to America, for who knows how long I shall remain there; but when I am in that very place, it is known to me and the providence of God. It shall be my task to serve and honor the reason therefore with love and cheerfulness, as long as I remain there. What otherwise remains to be mentioned, may be gleaned from several paragraphs of the *rationi peregrinandi;* of the present time. I therefore patiently commend the learned and beloved reader, to the faithful care of God in Christ and the word, and remain a fellow warrior, fellow sufferer, and fellow expectant of the body of Christ, which is scattered over the whole earth and await the coming of my chief shepherd and King with ardent longing.

DANIEL FALCKNER,
Citizen and Pilgrim of Pennsylvania
in Northern America.

PRÆMONITIO.

[PREFACE TO PRINTED VERSION.]

Wiewohlen unter denen mir vorgelegten Fragen einige Sachen sind, darumb ich mich dieselbigen, accurat zu wissen, in America nicht bekümmert, und deßwegen ich dieselbige biß auf weiteren Bescheid verspahren muß.

So will ich doch für diesesmal in einfältiger Liebe zu meinem Vatterlande, das mir Kundtbahre treuhertzig offenbahren, weilen zumahlen ich deßhalben zu meinen guten Freunden, durch GOttes Willen, aus dem fern-entlegenen Lande, aus der Ursache, wieder-gekehret bin, umb sie der grossen Wohlthaten GOttes und des wunderbaren Segens zu berichten der uff dieses neugebante Land in zeitlichen und himmlischen Gütern mit so voller reicher Hand geschüttet wird, da ich dann selbsten bey meiner hin- und her-Reise nichts anders beobachtet, als daß der Leib Christi erbauet werden möchte. Ich habe (hier und da) die Liebe zum Frieden getragen, die Schwachen gestärcket, die Müden ermuntert, die Fürwitzigen gestraffet, und mich mit denen in Hoffnung Lebenden erfreuet, auch sampt ihnen in denen Barbarischen Heydnischen Gräntzen ein aufrichtiges thätiges Christenthumb gefunden, welches ich meinen guten Freunden verkündiget, und gehe nun wieder dorthin, ob Gott will, Germaniam Novam Dei amantem & colentem in America zu sehen, und daselbst mich also zu bezeugen, wie es

(76)

PRÆMONITIO.

[PREFACE TO PRINTED VERSION.]

ALTHOUGH among the questions presented unto me there are some things concerning which I have not troubled myself to learn about in America. These I must reserve until I shall have further information. I will, however, for the present in artless simplicity to my fatherland candidly reveal that which is known unto me, as I have chiefly upon this account, by divine permission returned unto my good friends, from the far distant land, to acquaint them with the great beneficence of the Lord, and the wonderous blessings of both temporal and divine favors, which have been scattered, with so bountiful hand over this newly settled land, as during my journey to and fro, I have observed nought, but how the body of Christ is being built up. I have at least always contended in the interest of charity and peace, strengthened the weak hearted, encouraged the weary, corrected the froward, and rejoiced with those living in hope, also together I also found within the barbaric heathenish boundries, a sincere active Christianity which I proclaimed unto my good friends, and now return if it please God, to see again *Germaniam Novam Dei amantem and colentem in*

mein König der Könige von mir erfordert. Zu welcher vorhaben=
den Reise ich mich dem Gebete, und der Liebe aller wahren Glie=
der des Leibes JEsu empfohlen haben will. Ich bin aber darbey
gantz versichert, daß der HErr HErr mir meine Beylage bewahren
kan und will biß an jenen grossen Tag, deßwegen ich auch grosse
Freudigkeit gebrauche dem Tod und allem Verderben Trotz zu
bieten.

Ich protectire aber hiermit zum zierlichsten, daß ich nicht in=
tentionirt jemanden durch mein Kommen und wieder=weggehen,
oder durch mein Lobsprechen der Frommigkeit nnd Aufrichtigkeit
der neuen Christen in Pensylvania, in die Wüsten zu führen,
nein, sondern es gehe ein jeder zu Christo ; dessen die gantze Erde
ist, und all ihre Fülle, und lerne von ihm was er thun solle, wer
auß diesem Brunnen der Weißheit sich nicht erleuchten lässt, deme
ist weder von mir noch von einigem Menschen uff der Welt zu
helffen.

Die heutige Welt, und ihre Welt=Kinder in unserm Teutsch=
lande (nachdeme sie das liebe Christenthumb fast gar verlohren
und in eine Heucheley oder opus operatum verwandelt haben)
trösten sich zwar mit diesen Worten, sprechende: O es ist allezeit
böse gewesen, es war vor diesem auch so. Aber mein lieber
Landsmann weist du nicht daß die Axt dem Baume schon an die
Wurzel geleget ist, und daß der Baum, der keine gute Frucht
bringet, wird abgehauen und in das Feuer geworffen werden.
Darumb ist es hohe Zeit, daß man umbkehre, weil die Gnaden=
Thür noch offen stehet.

Es darff mir niemand nach America folgen, dann wer weiß,
wie lange ich da bin. Daß ich aber nicht hier, sondern lie=
ber all dorten bin, weiß ich und die treue Göttliche Providentz
Ursachen darfür, welchen in Freuden zu ehren und zu loben
mein Werck seyn wird, so lang ich lebe, und auch dort in alle
Ewigkeit.

Worzu ich dann auch den wohlgeneigten Leser hiermit noch=

America; and to testify there as my King of Kings
demands of me. For which proposed journey I will have
to commend myself to the love and prayers of all true
members of the body of Christ. I am, however, fully
assured, that the Lord of Lords, can and will protect my
mission until that great day. Therefore it is with great
joyfulness that I bid defiance unto death and all corruption.

I protest, however, herewith in the most graceful manner, that it is not my intention to lead anyone into these
deserts, by my coming and returning again, or by my
ecomium of the piety and sincerity of the new Christians
in Pennsylvania. No — rather let every one go unto
Christ, to whom belongs the whole earth, and the fullness
thereof, and learn from Him what he shall do. He that
doth not enlighten himself out of this fountain of wisdom,
is not to be helped by me or any person in the world.

The world of to-day and its worldly children in our
Germany (after they have almost entirely lost the dear
Christianity and have transformed it into a sham or *opus
operatum*) console themselves with these words, saying :

Oh! every age has been as bad as the present, formerly
it was even so. But my dear countrymen, do you not
know that the axe is already laid to the root of the tree,
and that the tree that doeth not bring forth good fruit, is
felled and cast into the fire. Therefore it is high time,
that one turneth, while yet the door of grace stands open.

No one need follow me to America, for who knows how
long I may remain there. But why I would rather be
there, than here, there are reasons therefore, known unto
me and the divine providence, which to honor and praise
in joyfulness shall be my task so long as I live, and also
beyond in all eternity.

Wherefore I then again heartily admonish the well dis-

mahlen hertzlich vermahne und der treuen GOttes-Hand in Christi
Liebe empfehle, und verbleibe

Der Mitkämpffende, Mitleydende, nnd
Mithoffende an dem Leibe JEsu,
eingepflantzte Mitknecht, erwartend
meines Ertz-Hirtens und Himmels-
Königs in sehnlichem Verlangen

Daniel Falckner, Bürger und Pilgrim in Pensylvanien in Norden
America.

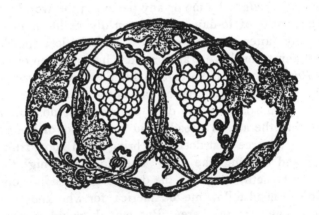

posed reader, and commend him unto the true guidance
of God in the love of Christ and remain

> The fellow warrior, fellow sufferer
> and fellow expectant of the body
> of Christ, an inveterate fellow
> servant, awaiting the coming of
> my chief shepherd, and Heav-
> enly King with ardent longing.
>
> Daniel Falckner, Citizen and Pil-
> grim in Pennsylvania in North-
> ern America.

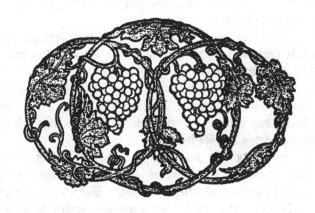

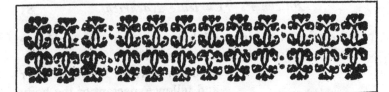

Die 1. Frage.

Wie die Reise nach America anzustellen?

Resp. Dese Frage begreifft zweyerley in sich. I. Den Weeg. II. Wie die Reise anzustellen [und auf was weise.] Von dem Ersten insonderheit, so mag derjenige, welcher Kosten wagen will, am gemächlichsten zu Lande von seiner Heimath nach Holland gehen, und sich grosser Pagage entschlagen.

Will man aber zu Wasser reisen, und mit dem geringsten Kosten, so gehet man nacher Hamburg oder Bremen, von dar mit Schiffen nach Engelland. [Es sey denn, dass man vorher durch Briefe berichtet Engellische Schiffe, die nach America zugehen entschlossen, allda antreffen könte.] Es wäre dann Sache daß man an nähern Orten Schiffe anträfe, die nach America zu gehen entschlossen.

Dann muß man mit dem Schiffer accordiren, daß derselbe einen mit allem bey sich habenden gen Philadelphiam in die Hauptstadt Pennsylvaniæ liefern müsse. Sollte aber eine neue Colonia in Sesquahanna Revier angeleget werden, so wäre es am besten vor den, der allda sich niederzulassen entschlossen, in der Bay von Marienland gantz oben in Bohemia Revier oder in Elck, das ist, Elends=Revier sich aussetzen liesse.

Weitläufftigen Haußrath muß man verkauffen, und in Engelland [und Holland] mit dem nothwendigsten davon wieder ver=

The 1st Question.

How to contrive for a voyage to America.

R. THIS question of the journey is a two-fold one; how to arrange for it, and upon what manner. Of the first he with whom expense is no object can go most comfortably by land from his home to Holland, and avoid the taking of any heavy baggage.

If any wish to go by water and with less expense, they can go by way of Hamburg or Bremen, thence by vessel to England, provided, however, that they have previously satisfied themselves by letter that the English ship sailing for America, in which it is proposed to take passage, will be met.[6] Next we must make our bargain with the skipper, so that he is bound to deliver us, with all our belongings, at Philadelphia, the capital of Pennsylvania.

Should, however, the new colony be founded on the Susquehanna river,[7] it would be best for such persons who wish or determine to settle there, to have themselves landed in the bay of Maria-land,[8] far up on the Bohemia river, or on the *Elk*, that is, *Elends river*.[9] Ordinary household furniture must be sold, and the most necessary

sehen. [So muss man auch kein Leinen ausgewaschenes und gebrauchtes mit nehmen, weil es schwere *Accise* in Engelland giebet]

Die ordentliche und beste Zeit ist im Früh=Jahr, im Aprill, und am Ende des Monats Augusti gegen Herbst, dieweilen umb dieselbe Zeit die meisten Ostwinde wehen, da muß man in London seyn. [wenn friede ist, gehen zwar Allezeit Schiffe] Allzu frühe im Frühlinge, und allzu spath im Herbst, ist es gar ungestümm im [auf dem] Meer.

Die 2. Frage.

Wie man sich auf der Reise zu verhalten?

R. **G**UT ist es, wann man ohne Rumor und Geräusch in Gottes Willen mit redlichem Abschied ausziehe, und auch also fort reise, damit man ein gutes Gewissen vor GOtt, und allen Menschen haben, und behalten mög, also nicht an einer Seite in die Versuchung der Forcht halber, an der andern Seite der Lust halber fallen und unterliegen möge. Darneben sey man schnell zu hören, und langsam zu reden. Im äusserlichen thue man alles ohne Zweiffeln und Murmeln, und lasse sich begnügen an dem, das da ist.

Die 3. Frage.

Wie man sich die Reise recht zu Nutze zu machen?

R. **G**Leichwie in Göttlicher Führung sich keine gewisse Theses oder Regeln machen lassen auf so, oder so, darumb [und deswegen] weil unsere Anschläge und Intention überall mit

articles be again purchased in England or Holland. Nor must any one take any linen, bleached or domestic, as this is subject to heavy custom duties in England.

The best and most suitable time for the voyage is in the spring, in April, and in the autumn toward the latter part of August, as during these times easterly winds prevail. Then we must be in London. In times of peace[10] ships sail at almost all seasons, yet if it is too early in the year, or late in the autumn, it is very boisterous upon the ocean.

The 2nd Question.

How to conduct oneself upon the voyage.

IT were well that one depart without bustle or excitement,[11] but with a righteous leavetaking in the fear of God, and thus set out, having and keeping a good conscience before God and all men; consequently not falling upon one side by the temptation of fear, nor falling and succumbing upon the other side by reason of pleasure. Moreover, be quick to hear, but slow to speak. In outward appearances do all things without doubting or complaint, and be content with what is there.

The 3rd Question.

How one may rightly turn the voyage to profit.

AS in divine guidance, no regular set thesis and rules "thus and so" can be given. For this reason, that as our intentions and efforts are tinged and encompassed

menschlicher Schwachheit so fern [Sie] durch die impressiones lauffen, umbgeben, also darff man nur stille und gelassen reisen wie die Kinder, die von einem Ort zum andern [getragen oder] gelaitet werden, und nur dasjenige insonderheit anmercken, worauf sie die treuführende Mutter weiset; So wird ein jeglicher Tag für das Seine sorgen, und der Nutzen wird [unserm mit Christo in Gott verborgenem Leben] zur Zeit der Offenbahrung Christi beygeleget.

Dann es verhält sich hier wie mit einigen Verrichtungen, welche gewissen Menschen umb ihres Besten [halber] willen anbefohlen sind. ex. gr. Einem Lahmen nutzet die Bewegung des schwachen Glieds. [Einem Lahmen ist die *Motion* oder bewegung des Schwachen Gliedes absonderlich gut] Einem andern nutzet das Gehen zur bessern Verdauung der Speisen, und zur gesunden Circulation des Geblüts. Ein Kauffmann machet profit von seiner Reise, wie es die Gelegenheit gibt.

Die 4. Frage.

Wie man in Specie uff der Reise sich zu seinem vorhabenden Zweck in Americam recht præpariren könne?

R. DJE Præparation so fern in sie die Moralität, oder in das Interesse der Seelen zielet, erhellet aus schon angeführten, und GOtt weiß am besten wie er einen jeglichen schon im Reisen noch zu fernern Reisen præpariren soll, zumahl insgemein die Menschen-Kinder also träges Hertzens sind, daß sie die Wichtigkeit einer Sache [und] ihres Vornehmens erst recht erkennen, wann sie dessenthalben [ernstlich] die Prob abzulegen gefordert werden. Eben wie die leichtsinnigen Knaben, welche erst anfangen zu lernen, wann sie nun auffagen sollen.

throughout with human weakness, so far as they flow through the sensuous impressions, therefore, we can only travel quietly and patiently, like unto children who are carried or led from one place to another, and who merely notice in particular that to which the true guiding mother calls attention. Thus each day will provide for itself, and the gain will be ours in the life hidden with Christ in God prepared for revelation. Now it is like the various actions which have been recommended to certain people for their benefit. Thus, to a lame one a motion or movement of the weak member is specially grateful; to another, walking gives a better digestion of the food and a healthful circulation of the blood. A merchant maketh profit from his journey as opportunity offers.

The 4th Question.

How may one rightly prepare himself during the voyage for his intended purpose in America?

THE preparation, so far as morality or the interest of the soul is concerned, appears from what has already been presented. God knows best how to prepare everyone upon the voyage for a future journey, as generally the children of men are of a slothful nature, so that they fail to realize the importance of matters and their understanding until they are called upon to give some earnest proof upon that account, even as the frivolous youth, who only begin to study when they are called upon to stop.

Inzwischen ist wohl gethan, wann man sich dienstfertig, ver=
gnüglich und Arbeitsam gewöhne, damit man hernach sich nicht
in offerbare falsche Absichten verwickele, sondern GOtt und Men=
schen getreue sey in der Aufrichtigkeit. Im äusserlichen ist gut,
daß man in Holland oder Engelland, nach dem Vermögen, das
GOtt in seinem Segen darreichet, versehe mit Kleidern, Betten,
Eisenwerck, und nothdürfftigem Haußrathe.

Diejenige Wahren so in Pensylvanien mitzunehmen dienlich:

Holländische und Osnabrückische Leinwat, Holländischen Zwirn,
Bremer Laylacken, davon man erst in Engelland Nachricht ein=
holen muß, ob mans in Holland einladen darff, und wie hoch der
Accis ist; Gewalckte Strümpffe; Einige gute Scheermesser,
Schlachtmesser, Schnittmesser, breite Beiler, allerhand Maisel
und Failen. Grabscheid, Schauffeln, Sensen, Gabeln, Sicheln,
Sägen, und Hämmer, und eiserne Pott und Kesseln, wie auch
kleine Kupferne Kesselein, allerhand gering Wollenzeug vor Kin=
der=Kleider und Unterfutter. Einige Madrazzen, und bundte
Halstücher, Catoen und Barchet. Allerhand Koch=Gewürtz.
Fenster=Bley. Kraut und Loth, auch allerhand Schrot und
Hagel=Dunst zum Vögel schiessen.

Die 5. Frage.
Wofür man sich uff der Reise zu hüten?

R. DASS man sich durch die vielfältigen Objecta nicht allzu=
sehr distrahiren lasse, noch [durch] die mancherley
Gesellschaften, und unterschiedliche Conversationen, welche man

In the meantime it will be well for one to accustom himself to be obliging, pleasant, and industrious, that he may not become entangled in false positions, but remain true in all sincerity unto God and mankind. In outward matters it is well for one to purchase in Holland and England such clothing, bedding, ironware and necessary household goods, according to the means with which the blessing of God hath endowed him.

Such goods as will be of service if taken to Pennsylvania.

Dutch and Osnabrück Linens, Holland Thread, Bremen bed-sheets, whereof one must first get information from England, if they can be loaded in Holland, and how high the tariff is. Fulled stockings, several good razors, butcher's knives, chopping knives, broad-axes, all sorts of chisels and files, spades, shovels, scythes, forks, sickles, saws, hammers, iron pots and kettles, also small copper kettles, all kinds of cheap woollen goods for children's wear and linings. Several mattresses, colored kerchiefs, calico and canton flannel, all kinds of cookery spices, glazier's lead, powder and shot, also all sizes of shot and dust shot to shoot birds.

The 5th Question.

What one has to beware of on the voyage?

ONE should not permit himself to be detracted too much by the many outward things, nor by the mixed company and the different conversations (which one

nicht allezeit wählen [oder wo sie bösse sind nach seinem willen] noch vermeiden kann, [doch auch zu seinem nactheil nicht unterhalten soll.] Dem Leibe gebe man ordentlich seine Speise und sehe sich wohl für, daß man sich vor unreinem Trinkge= schirr und Betten, [und Gesellschaft] so viel möglich, verwahre.

Die 6. Frage.

Was man uff dem Schiffe [wegen umgang] mit denen Schiffleuten in Acht zu nehmen?

R. DAS Schiff=Volck muß man in seinem Thun lassen, und sich nicht allzugemein machen, [Es sey denn dass einen Gott sonderlich bey einem oder anderm einen eingang machte;] insonderheit haben sich Weibs=Personen in Acht zu nehmen. Man muß respectiren den Schiff=Capitän, den Steuer= mann, Bootsmann, Koch und Keller. [Den Koch, Kellner, Bothsmann zusamt den Schiff-Capitain und Steuermann muss man so viel als möglich zu Freunden behalten] In specie muß man sich einen geringen Schiffmann zum guten Freunde machen, mit Versprechung eines Tranckgelds oder Brand= weingelds, [darneber einen gemeinen Schiffmann durch Verheissung eines Trinckgeldes oder dann und wann durch mittheilung eines trunks Brantwein an sich halten] damit man, zu harten Sturms=Zeiten oder bey vorfallender Schiffs= Kranckheit sich seiner Aufwartung getrösten könne. Das Seinige muß ein jeglicher wohl verwahren, und nicht unachtsam liegen lassen, damit einiges böses Schiff=Volck nicht Gelegenheit zum stehlen bekomme. An denen Oertern auf dem Schiffe, wo das Schiff=Volck seine Verrichtungen hat, muß man sich nicht viel auf= halten.

cannot select at all times, nor avoid as we would desire where they are evil) nor should one enter into any amusement to his own detriment. Give unto the body its proper food, and so far as possible beware of unclean drinking vessels, bedding and company.

The 6th Question.

What one has to be mindful of in his intercourse with the sailors and crew?

THE crew must be left alone in their ways and doings, neither must one fraternize with them, unless it be that the Lord has made a special enlightment in one or another of them. Females, in particular, have to be careful of themselves. It is well for one to keep on as friendly terms as possible with the ship's-cook, steward, boatswain, as well as with the captain and mate. The favor of the common sailor should be gained by the promise of a gratuity or an occasional drink of brandy, so that one may depend upon their attention in stormy or heavy weather, or during sea-sickness. Every one must carefully guard his personal property, and allow nothing to lie around, so as not to offer to the wicked ship's crew any incentive for stealing. One should not spend much time in the crew's house of office.

Die 7. Frage.

Was wegen der Schiffs- oder See-Krankheiten in Acht zu nehmen?

R. Die [schiffs] Krankheit überfällt insgemein die Gallsüch= tige, oder zum Schwindel geneigte, und forchtsame Gemü= ther. [am meisten] Dahero wäre es gut, daß man sein Gemüth [Durch hohere Gedanken zu ordnen] vorhero zu ruhigen Sedaten Gedanken disponire, den Leib aber per purgantia reinige; [und das natürliche gebrechen der Schwindelhaff= tigen und furchtsamen Natur sich auf einer Schaukel zu benehmen] Die Forcht sich zu benehmen, zu vorhero uff kleinen [wasser in einem] Kahnen fahren lerne, die Phantasey [zu beugen und] durch eine anwachsende Christliche Ubung, und muthig und kühne werden lerne. [also gar, das worfür immer ein welt Mensch nicht erschrickt auch ein Gott und Tugend liebender Mensch dasselbige keinesweges zu fürchten hat] Dann worfür ein böser Welt=Mensche erschrickt, darfür hat sich ein frommer GOtt= und Tugendliebender Mensche gar nichts zu förchten.

Und ist auch zu observiren, daß wo man starke Winde und Höhle der See vermercket, man sich nit mit Speise vorher über= lade, sondern nur ein wenig Zwyback un Brandewein zu sich nehme, sich in sein Bette niederlege, und auf der Seiten liegen bleibe, biß man der Motion des Schiffs besser gewohne. Man kan sich auch ein Tag oder acht, [nacht] ehe man zur See gehet, auf das Schiff begeben damit man des Wassers und der See= Lufft gewohne.

The 7th Question.

What is to be observed concerning ship or sea-sickness ?

SEA-SICKNESS chiefly affects persons of a bilious disposition or such as are inclined to vertigo or fear. Therefore, it is best to occupy one's mind with higher thoughts [12] and to cleanse the body; while such as suffer from dizziness or are of a timorous nature should betake themselves to a swing or a little boat upon smaller waters, so as to overcome the fantasy of fear, and by increasing the practice of Christian virtues, become bold and courageous, so that as God-loving and virtue-loving persons they will in no manner have to fear, that which fails to frighten a worldly-minded person. It is also to be observed that when we meet with strong winds and high seas, one must not overload himself with food, but rather content himself with a little zwieback [13] and brandy, and lie down in bed upon the right side, and remain there until one is better accustomed to the motion of the vessel. One may also go aboard the ship for a day or night prior to sailing, so as to get accustomed to the water and the sea-air.

Die 8. Frage.

Was junge Leute, die dahin reisen wollen, zu observiren haben?

[Wie junge Leute, die einmahl dahin gehen sollen auf solche weise dazu zu *præpariren* seyn?

R. WAS bereits auf die 4te Frage geantwortet, und wie diejenigen Regeln in Acht zu nehmen sind, welche man sonst denen in die Frembd Reisenden zu geben pflegt, doch nur so fern, als sie dem wahren Christenthumb, und der wahren Tugend gemäß sind.

Die 9. Frage.

Was bei der Ankunfft in Pensylvania oder Virginia zu observiren?

R. DAS Erste und nöthigste ist, dem HErrn seinem GOtt, der durch Wasser und Feuer führet, einen Danck-Altar in der stillen Verborgenheit seines Hertzens aufzurichten, und in gutem Vorsatze [demselben] seine Gelübde zu bezahlen. Darneben sehe man sich nach [einem oder mehr] guten Freunden umb, denen man seine Anschläge, wie und was Lebens-Art man führen wolle, entdecke. Man stehe ja nicht auf seinem Kopffe, sondern lasse sich durch die Erfahrung anderer zu seinem Besten rathen, inzwischen hat man sich nicht zu übereilen, vielmehr mit Gedult der Göttlichen Schickung abzuwarten, biß man sich besser [völlig] in die Art des Landes einrichten lerne.

The 8th Question.

How young persons, who intend going there for any specific purpose, are to be properly prepared.

THE answer to this question already appears in those previously set forth, in particular in *Question IV*. Herewith one may observe such rules as are usually given to itinerant journeymen, though only so far as they conform with true Christianity and virtue.

The 9th Question.

What is to be observed upon the arrival in Pennsylvania or Virginia?

FIRST and above all, raise up unto the Lord, who hath guided you safely through fire and water, an altar of thankoffering in the inmost recesses of your heart, with a firm resolution to pay unto him your vows. At the same time seek to make one or more good friends, to whom you can disclose your intentions, projects and manner of living. Do not stand upon your own head, but take advice from the experience of others. In the mean time one need not act hastily, but await with patience the Divine dispensation, until one learns fully how to establish oneself according to custom of the country.

Die 10. Frage.

Wie man sich vorsichtiglich gegen die mancherley Secten dort verhalten solle?

R. DAS ist eine schwere Frage, und fast unmöglich zu beantworten, noch schwerer zu practiciren, doch weil die Lauterkeit des Glaubens JEsu in der Einfalt die Gerechtigkeit der Völcker erfüllet, so thut man darinn den Secten [keinen grösseren] noch den meisten Eintrag, und zwar nach ihrer eigenen Anforderung, und mit ihrem Consens. Dann wann man sich in der That so fromm gegen sie bezeuget, wie sie in einem gesetzlichen Weege verlangen, und doch darbey nicht stoltz ist, und vielmehr [in der Freundlichkeit und Liebe ihnen etwas Lebendiges bey aller Gelegenheit bezeuget] ihnen Freundlichkeit, und Liebe bezeuget.

Die 11. Frage.

Wie man sich dorten am besten einrichten könne zur Haußhaltung?

[zur information, zur Haus-Arbeit, zur Haushaltung]

R. [DIESE Einrichtung kan geschehen] Nach der Erkanntnuß eines jeglichen Gabe, und nach seiner resolution in den Göttlichen Willen, ingleichen [wie schon oben gemeldet] nach eines jeglichen Mittel und Vermögen mag er seine [wer etwas hat kan sich mit nöthigen zur] Haußhaltung mit dienlichen Dingen versehen. Wer aber nichts hat [sehe nur das er frei und ohne Schuld überkomt und lasse den lieben Gott sorgen *ipse faciet*] und doch Sprachen kan, der kan [in den

The 10th Question.

How to conduct oneself there circumspectly and inoffensively toward the divers sects.

THIS is a difficult question, and one almost impossible to answer, and still harder to observe. Nevertheless, as the clearness of the faith of Jesus in its simplicity imbues the nations with righteousness, consequently we can offer to the sects no greater encouragement and indeed this according to and with their consent, than when we always and in a lawful manner show ourselves actually as devout as they demand, and yet be not proud, but rather extend unto them friendliness and love, thus showing vital Christianity upon opportunity.

The 11th Question.

How best to establish oneself, and concerning information about domestic affairs and the household.

THE establishment can be done according to the knowledge of every one's endowment, and according to their fortitude in divine providence, as has already been previously mentioned, according to every person's means and ability. Those who have any means can supply themselves with the necessary household utensils. Such as have nothing, let them see that they come over free and without debt, and let the good Lord provide (*ipse faciet*).

Städten] offentliche Schulen anstellen, und dann den lieben GOtt sorgen lassen, ipse faciet. [Die *information* betreffend, so muss dieselbe *privatim* in einzelnen Häusern meistentheils geschehen, weil die Teutschen allda noch nicht in einer eigenen *Colonie* zusammen Verfasset wohnen. Wer mehr sprachen gelernt hat als eine, kan in den Städten offentliche Schulen anstellen. Bey der Landschule ist zu beobachten, dass man die Kinder wo sie tüchtig der Hülfe der Eltern nicht entbehren können, deswegen man morgens und abendszeit in acht zu nehmen hat, oder sie wechselweise von ihren Verrichtungen zu sich rufet, ja bey denen Verrichtungen selbst mit ihnen *conversiret* und acht hat, ob und wie treulich sie ein Ding thun.]

Die 12. Frage.

Was der Gesundheit wegen dort zu observiren?

R. DIE Abwechslung von Hitze in die Kälte, und von der Kälte in die Wärme, [ist bisweilen schnell, dahero es] verursachet bey zarten Constitutionen Winde [verkältung Heischerkeit] Heiterkeit, Schnuppen und Obstructiones, und dieses so vielmehr, weilen durch den [vielen und] täglichen Gebrauch der süssen Sachen, als Syrupp, Zucker, Indianisch Korn [Brantwein, von Zucker-Rieth] Liquor [Brantewein] von Pfirschen, Melonen und dergleichen, der ohne das durch die Verwechslung des Temperaments causirte und unordentliche Appetit gestärcket, die kalte Säure vermehret, und allerhand Zufälle verursacht werden, dahero sonderlich unter unordentlichen wohllüstigen Gemütern entstehen folgende Kranckheiten, als Magen=Fieber, Miltz=Fieber, Gallen=Kranckheiten, Colica, Dis-

Concerning information, this must be chiefly obtained privately in the several houses, as the Germans as yet do not live together there as a distinct colony. Those who have learned more languages than one, can open a public school in the city. In the country schools it is, however, to be noted, that where the parents cannot spare the actual services of their children, the spare time in the mornings and evenings must be taken into consideration, or one may call them from their duties in turns; yea, even converse with them while they are at work, at the same time paying attention that they are diligent and properly perform their duties.

The 12th Question.

What is to be observed regarding one's health?

THE variations from heat to cold and from cold to warmth are often sudden; consequently it causes, in delicate constitutions, flatulence, colds, hoarseness, catarrhal fever and obstructions, all of which are accelerated by the daily and plentiful use of sweet things, such as syrup, sugar, Indian corn, brandy from sugar cane (rum), brandy from peaches, melons and the like, which tend to increase the disordered digestion resulting from a change of temperature, increasing the gastric acid, thereby bringing about all kinds of conditions and attacks of illness. Therefore, dissolute and lustful dispositions are especially liable to such disorders as gastric and splenetic fevers, bilious complaints, colic, dysentery, pleurisy and similar

senteria [Pleuritis] **und dergleichen.** [Die Kinder muss man ordentlich im Essen halten, sonst brüten sie leicht würmer, zumal da man der milch häufig gebrauchet. Die Brust und die Kähle muss man in Schweiss gegen die kühlen Lüftlein verwahren.] **Darumb iſt nicht dienlich viel Saltz-Speiſſen eſſen** [zumahl wenn man der starken Englischen Biere, Brantewein und Apfel-Trank zugleich mit sich nimmt] **bey dem Getranck des ſtarcken Engliſchen Biers und Brantenweins. Die abwechßlende** [Motion] **Commotion iſt ſehr gut, lange ſchlaffen aber iſt ſchädlich, wie auch das Liegen und Sitzen uff der** [blossen] **Erden, weil ſie ſehr nitroſiſch iſt, und daß ichs kurtz** [sage] **faſſe: Das Land will keinen** Debou- chanten [oder] **und Faullentzer vertragen, ſondern befördert ihn bald zu ſeinem Grabe.**

Die 13. Frage.

Wie die Luft dort Winters- und Sommers-Zeit beſchaf- fen?

R. [**D**IE Luft] **Sie iſt faſt eben wie hier, denen Jahrs-Zeiten nach, nur daß ſie überall viel subtiler und penetranter iſt, und ob ſchon die Sonne mehr Gewalt hat, ſo thun doch die Winde ihren Strahlen Eintrag. Von 9. Uhr Morgens biß umb Glocke 2. iſt es im Sommer am wärmſten, inſonderheit im Monat** Julio und Augusto. **Zwo Stunden vor Abends beginnet es insgemein kühle und feuchte zu werden, und thauet die Nacht über ſehr ſtarck, wo aber dieſer Thau eine Nacht auſſen bleibt, ſo iſt es ein Zeichen, daß es bald regnen werde. Starcke Winde wehen aus Weſten und Nord-Weſten** [davon der letztere eben- das jenige wetter mit sich bringet was hier bey uns der Nordostwind thut, hingegen bringet uns der Nordost und

diseases. Children's diet must be carefully attended to, or else they easily breed worms, particularly as much milk is frequently used. The chest and throat, when in a perspiration, must be carefully guarded against the cool breezes. Too much salt food is not advisable, particularly when one partakes at the same time of the strong English beer, and apple beverages.[14] Occasional exercise is very beneficial. To sleep long is harmful, nor is it well to sit or lie upon the bare earth, as the ground is very nitrous, and that I may express myself plainly: the country will not endure any bacchanalian or idle sluggard, but quickly sends them to their grave.

The 13th Question.

How the climate is constituted there in summer and winter.

THE climate is almost the same as here, according to the season, only that everywhere it is much more subtle and penetrating. Although the sun has greater power, yet the breezes temper its rays. In summer it is warmest from nine o'clock in the morning until the clock strikes two, particularly during the months of July and August. Two hours before nightfall it generally begins to get cool and damp. During the night the dew falls heavily. Whenever the dew fails to fall, it is a sign that it will soon rain. Strong winds blow from the west and northwest, of which the latter brings the same kind of weather as the northeast winds do with us. On the con-

Ostwind einen zweitägigen treibenden regen, der Sudost-
wind einen zwölf Stündigen Sturm und Regen] **der Sud=
wind bringet einen Platzregen und groß Gewässer.** [Im winter
hat die Sonne mehr Kraft als hier, deswegen der schnee
nach und nach vergehet, darzu hilft auch dass der kürtzeste
Tag bey uns über 2 Stunden länger gleich wie der längste
um so viel kürtzer. Die grösste kälte ist mit Nordwest-
wind, da es in einer Nacht mehr gefrieret als sonst in
zweyen] **Der kürzeste Tag ist 2. Stunde länger, und der Längste
2. Stunde kürzer.**

Die 14. Frage.

Von der Fertilität des Landes?

R. **D**iese [Die *Fertilität* des Landes] **ist köstlich, und deß
Korn=Bau halber mit** [einigen orten der Pfaltz der
güldenen Aue] **dem Magdeburgischen und Halberstädtischen
Lande zu vergleichen, nur daß mehr Krafft und Stärcke** [allda
ist] **allhier, als in Teutschlande ist, dahero auch alle Dinge durch
einen schnellen Trieb wachsen, und noch einst so reichlich Früchte
[wo nicht mehr geben] geben.**

Die 15. Frage.

Was das Land für Früchte und Gewächse gebe?

R. **S**o **wohl Teutsch Korn** [Das Land giebt alles Korn so
man hier zu Lande hat nebst dem] **als Indianisch
Korn von allerley** [unterschiedlicher] **Art** [und dergleichen]
Bohnen [und] **Erbsen** [nächst dem wilden Reis wohl

trary, the northeast winds and easterly winds bring us a two days' driving rain; southeasterly winds, a twelve hour storm and rain; and the south wind, sudden and heavy showers and down pours of rain. During the winter the sun has greater strength than here; consequently snow gradually disappears. Another advantage is that the shortest day with us is two hours longer,[15] while the longest is so much shorter. The greatest cold comes with the northwest wind, when it freezes harder in one night than otherwise in two.

The 14th Question.

Regarding the fertility of the country.

THE fertility of the country is excellent, and the culture of grain vies with several parts of the Palatinate, and may be compared to the fertile golden meadows of the Magdeburg and Halberstadt districts, only that here there is more force and strength, whereby all things grow with a more rapid energy, and give one a second harvest, just as plentiful, if not more.

The 15th Question.

Of the sorts of fruits and vegetables the country produces.

THE country produces all kinds of cereals similar to what we have here,[16] together with Indian corn of different kinds, and similar beans and peas. Possibly rice may also be cultivated. Peas, kitchen vegetables, pump-

wachsen] Linsen, Reiß, Hanff, Lein, Hopffen, allerhand Garten=Früchte [gedeyen wohl und bezahlen dem, der ihrer pfleget seine arbeit reichlich] zahme Obst=Bäume [lassen sich geschwinde anbauen, dass ein Haus-Vater der Früchte davon in 7 Jahren geniessen kan] Pfirschen, Kirschen, [sind gar reichlich dasselbst und vermehren sich selbst wie Un-kraut] Aepffel, Birnen, Kastanien, [und] Nußbäume, [deren drey bis vierley art] Cedern, [dreierley Art] Eichen, Eschen, Saffafraß, Pappeln, Mespeln, Tannen, Buchen und dergleichen, [In Verginien und Marie-Land hat man ein hartes und lange dauerndes Holtz *Cocus* genant ingleichen Cypressen, und wie man sagt] auch hat man weiter hinein das Lignum Guajacum oder Sanctum.

Die 16. Frage.

Wie sich allda die Europäer nähren?

R. WElche unter ihnen kein Handwerck treiben können, die nähren sich von dem Ackerbau und von Viehezucht. Einige treiben Indianische Handelschafft, oder lassen sich zur Schiffahrt gebrauchen

Die 17. Frage.

Von denen Wilden, ihren Nationen, Anzahle, und Sprache?

R. DIE Nationen der Wilden sind mancherley, doch sind uns nur diejenigen bekannt, die umb uns wohnen, die andern kommen nicht in unser Gesichte, deren Nahmen, Herkunfft, Wei=

kins, melons, roots, hemp, flax, hops, and all other sorts
of garden produce flourish and recompense such as cultivate them richly for their labor. Domesticated fruit trees
mature quickly, so that the husbandman can enjoy the
fruit therefrom within seven years. Peaches and cherries
are plentiful here and increase spontaneously like weeds.
Of forest trees we have the Chestnut and three or four
varieties of nutbearing trees. Of cedar trees there are
three varieties; there are also Oak, Ash, Sassafras, Poplar,
Medlar,[17] Beech and the like. In Virginia and Maryland
they have a hard wood called Cocas,[18] also Cypress and it
is said further in the interior lignum guaiacum[19] or sanctum.

The 16th Question.

How the Europeans support themselves, and the
various ways in which they earn their livelihood.

THE Europeans who have no trade support themselves
chiefly by agriculture and breeding cattle. Some
follow trading with the Indians or find employment with
the shipping.

The 17th Question.

Of the savages, their nations, numbers and
languages.

THERE are many nations among the savages. Only
such, however, are known to us as live about us.
The others we do not get sight of. Their names, origin,

sen und Sitten sollen zu einer andern Zeit, so GOtt will, und
wir leben, erfolgen. Ihre Anzahl vermindert sich gewaltig, in=
dem sie durch die Kranckheiten der Europäer angestecket dahin
gerissen werden, daß wo man derselben vor 30. Jahren 100
[200] und mehr gesehen, itzo [man nun] kaum einen siehet,
So viel Nationen bey ihnen sind, so vielerley und gantz unter=
schieden sind auch die [derselben] Sprachen.

Die 18. Frage.

Wie mit ihnen umbzugehen?

R. [DER umbgang mit ihnen] In eusserlichen Affairen
ist noch [leiblich] wohl mit ihnen umbgehen. In
ihren Humor muß man sich beugen, und ihre Zuneigunge suchen,
dann in ihrer Art stehen sie feste, sie thun, reden und sehen aus,
gleich wie sie gesinnet sind. Die Einfalt, mit [zahmen *Creaturen*] ihnen umbzugehen ist, [in dem umbgang mit ihnen]
die beste Staats=Regel. Wann sie truncken sind [oder dazu
lust und Gelegenheit haben,] so ist das beste, sie zu meiden.

Die 19. Frage.

Was ihre Tugenden und Laster seyen?

R. IHRE Tugend aller Tugenden ist, die Unverdrossenheit,
demjenigen nachzustreben, was sie sich vorgesetzet, sie sind
natürlich einfältig, dahero [auch wo sie Verstand und] wo sie
Mühe beweisen, thun sie es doch nicht umb ein solches Interesse,
davon sie einen beständigen profit und Nutzen vor sich zu machen

manners and habits will follow at some future time. So God wills, and we live. They decrease in numbers rapidly, as they become infected [20] with the diseases of the Europeans and are swept away. Where thirty years ago one could see two hundred or more, one can now hardly find a single one. As many nations as there are, so entirely different are their languages.

The 18th Question.

How to establish intercourse with them?

THE intercourse with them in outward affairs is still moderate. One must bow to their humor, and seek their favor. For in their opinions they stand firm, and speak and look just as they are disposed. Simplicity is the best public law in intercourse with tame creatures. When they are drunk, or have any desire and opportunity thereto, it is best to avoid them.

The 19th Question.

What are their virtues and vices?

THEIR virtue of all virtues is their perseverance in striving after what they resolve upon. They are by nature unsophisticated. Therefore where they show intellect and effort they do not do it with an intention, whereby they expect to reap any permanent benefit or

gedächten, sondern nur daß sie sich selbst eine Satisfaction geben, und darfür angesehen seyn wollen, daß sie auch etwas thun können. Wiewohlen auch viele die Liebe zum starcken Geträncke, und die Begierde, bessere Kleidunge zu haben [und andere dergleichen Dinge wie *inventios* und fleissig] sie eigennutzig [und] Gewinnsüchtig machet. Sie sind insgemein Sociabel, freygebig, ernsthafftig [welche ernsthafftigkeit bissweilen mit Argwohn und] mit Zorn vermischet, sonderlich gegen ihres gleichen.

Die 20. Frage.

Wie sie wohnen? und wie weit die Hütten von einander?
[seyn]

R. SIE wohnen bald hier bald dar nachdem sie ihr Sinn und ihre Lust treibet, doch haben [sie] auch einige beständige Oerter, da viele Hütten stehen, [auch einige] wie Städte, welche doch weder denen Hütten, noch denen andern Umbständen nach, von jenen viel unterschieden sind.

Die 21. Frage.

Wie sich die Wilden nehren?

R. DAS vornehmste von ihren Nahrungs=Mitteln, ist das Jagen und Fischen, und darneben pflantzen ihre Weiber ein wenig Indianisch Korn, Bohnen, Kürbse, Melonen [Quashies] und dergleichen ꝛc.

profit for themselves, but merely to give themselves the satisfaction to be considered able to accomplish something ; although now the love for strong drink and the desire for better garments and other similar things makes them desirous and industrious, but also selfish and greedy. In general for trifles they are sociable, liberal, and earnest; an earnestness which is often mixed with suspicion and anger, especially against their equals.

The 20th Question.

How they live, and what distance their cabins are apart.

THEY live, sometimes here, sometimes there, according as their inclination or fancy moves them. Yet they have some permanent places, where there are many cabins, also some towns, in which, however, neither the cabins nor other conditions differ greatly from the others.

The 21st Question.

How they support themselves.

THEIR principal means of existence is derived from hunting and fishing. In addition their women plant a little Indian corn, beans, pumpkins, melons, squash, and such like.

Die 22. Frage.
Wie sie den Tag zubringen?

————

R. [DIESES erhället meistentheils schon aus vorher-
gehender Beantwortung, welcher noch dieses
beyzufügen] Wie erst gedacht, mit Jagen und Fischen, etliche
bereiten auch Felle, [Manns-Arbeit ist Fell bereiten, von
welchen sie hernach Strümpfe, Hemden und Sipax, das
ist Schuhe machen] machen Strümpffe und Sigax, das ist,
Schuhe, item Höltzerne Schüsseln und Löffel, von Knotten, die
an den Bäumen wachsen. [Und was etwa sonst zu ihren zeuge
gehöret] Die Weiber hauen Holtz, Kochen, warten der Kinder,
machen Beutel von wilden Hanff, [welchen sie *Notis* nennen]
auch Stricke. Item Tapezereyen von gefärbtem Strohe, Körbe
von gefärbtem Bast, und Decken von Federn geflochten.

————

Die 23. Frage.
Wie sie ihre Kinder erziehen?

————

R. DIE Jungen lernen von [sich] selbst thun wie die Alten,
welche sie durch Lob und Liebkosen, als wie junge Affen
gewöhnen, daher die Kinder sehr freundlich sind. Und gleichwie
die Eltern alles mit Lust und gutem Willen thun, also siehet
man, daß auch Kinder zeugen und auferziehen bey ihnen keine
Beschwerde ist, man findet auch nicht leicht ein krippelhafftes und
verwarlostes Kind unter ihnen. Vide plura infra in der 72.
Frage.

The 22nd Question.

How men, women and children spend the day.

———

THIS is shown for the most part in the preceding answers; to which we may add that it is the work of the men to prepare the skins, from which they afterwards make stockings, shirts and Sipax, that is shoes.[21] Item, wooden bowls and spoons they make out of the knots that grow on the trees, and what else belongs to their implements. The women cook, chop wood, attend to the children, make bags out of wild hemp,[22] which they call *notis*, ropes, tapestry from dyed straw, baskets from the coloredinner bark of trees, and braid feathers into rugs.

———

The 23rd Question.

How do they rear their children?

———

THE young learn of themselves to do just as their seniors do; for which, just as young monkeys, they receive great praise and much caressing. Therefore the children are very affable.

Die 24. Frage.

Wie sie sich verheurathen? quibus Ceremoniis? und ob sie Polygami?

———

R. **D**ISES geschicht [so viel mir bekannt] noch mit ziemlichen Umbständen und Ordnung, und ist zu verwundern, daß weniger Unkeuschheit unter ihnen zu vermercken, da sie doch meistens nackend gehen, und allezeit Gelegenheit darzu haben, dahingegen [als unter unsern] bey uns Europäischen Völckern [allwo die Schärffigkeit der Gesetze, Gottes Befehl zu geschweigen] die Schärffe der weltlichen Obrigkeit des ernsten Befehls Gottes zu geschweigen, die Menschen aber doch nicht so fromm machen und erhalten können, als wie jene ohne Gesetze sind. Die Heuraths Ceremonien bey ihnen sind also: Der Mann gibt der Frauen einen Hirsch-Fuß, welches bedeutet, daß er ihr Fleisch verschaffen will. Die Frau gibt dem Manne eine Hand voll Korn [oder Gewächsse] welches bedeutet, daß sie vor das Brod und Küche sorgen wolle. Einem Manne ist [vergönnt] erlaubet zwo Frauen zu nehmen, wann er sie zu ernähren gedencket, sonst ist es ihme eine grosse Schande. [*Sed non vice versa.* Von einigen wird gesaget, dass nachdem eine Dirne an einen gewissen Mann versprochen, sie hernach, ehe er sie heim holet, Freiheit habe um sich etwas zu verdienen, *ut quaestum de corpore facitat*, welches ich aber nicht gewiss weiss]

The 24th Question.

How do they marry, with what ceremonies;[23] and whether they are polygamous.[24]

***

THIS is the case, so far as is known to me; still, with suitable formality and order; and it is a marvel that less immorality is to be found among them (although they almost always go naked, and have at all times greater opportunity thereto), than among our European people, where the severity of the laws, to say nothing of the Divine command, cannot make the people as upright, and keep them so, as those who are entirely without any laws.

The marriage ceremony is as follows: The man gives the woman a deer's foot, which signifies that he will keep her supplied with meat. The woman gives the man a handful of corn or vegetables, which imports that she will look after his bread and cooking. One man is permitted to have two wives if he can support them, otherwise it is a great reproach to them; but not vice versa. By some it is said that after a wench is engaged to a certain man, she is afterwards, before he takes her home, at liberty to earn something for herself, *ut quaestum di corpore faciat*, which I however do not know for certain.

Die 25. Frage.[1]
Von der Wilden ihrer Sprache und Umbgang?

R. SOLCHE ist leicht zu erlernen, dieweil sie nicht mehr Wörter, als Dinge haben. Ihre Verba und Nomina haben weder Tempora noch Numerum; die andern sind lauter Nomina propria und appellativa. In Ermanglung der Copularum, haben sie einige von denen Schweden und andern angenommen, e. g. Ok. und Ni. Das R. können sie nicht aussprechen. Sie reden mehr mit ihren Geberden und mit dem Affect, dann mit den Worten, dahero der jenige, dermit ihnen redet, und das, worvon er redet, gegenwärtig seyn muß. Als: Lanconti sagen sie, wann sie einem etwas geben wollen, oder wan sie etwas gegeben haben wollen, sie können keine Vielheit in ihren Gedancken leyden, und excoliren mehr das Studium oblivionis, als Scientiæ & Memoriæ, darumb haben sie auch keine Monumenta antiquitatis unter sich. Wann aber etwas unter ihne solle gedacht und behalten werde, so nehmen sie ihr junges Volck zusammen, und bedeuten es ihnen, und wann sie es der Mühe werth achten, so befehlen sie denenselben, daß sie es in ihrem hohen Alter ihren Jungen wieder befehlen, und eindrucken mögen. In ihrem Umbgang muß man sich nach ihrem Humeur richten, und seine Freundlichkeit und Lachen mit Ernsthaftigkeit vermischen, weilen sie argwöhnisch sind und leicht gedencken, daß man sie verachte. Umb völlig Vertrauen bey ihnen zu erlangen und zu erhalten, ist es gut, daß man sie zu unserer Wohnunge kommen lasse, sie nicht ohne Essen und Tranck gehen lasse, und ihnen bisweilen etwas vorschiesse an Pulver, Bley, Taback. Und wo sie zu Abends kommen, ihnen Freyheit anbiete, bey dem Feuer zu liegen, wann man dann wieder zu ihnen kommt, so sind sie desto liebreicher und Gastfreyer.

1 Not in original MSS.

The 25th Question.

[Not in the original MSS.]

Of the Savages, their language and intercourse.

SUCH is easy to acquire, as they have no more words than things. Their verbs and nouns have neither tense nor numbers. The others are all proper names and appellatives. In the absence of conjunctives they have adopted several from the Swedes and others ex. gr. Ok and Ni.

They cannot pronounce the letter R. They speak more with gestures and their effect than with words, therefore, anyone who speaks with them, and that about which he speaks must be present. Thus they say *Laconti*, when they want to give one something, or when they want something given to them, they cannot endure any multiplicity in their ideas, and cultivate more the study of forgetfulness than that of knowledge and memory. Therefore, they have no monuments of antiquity among them. But when anything amongst them is to be commemorated and retained, they gather their young people together and explain it unto them, and when they deem it important enough, they command them, that in their old age they again impart and impress it upon the youth.

In their intercourse, one must conform to their disposition, and blend his affability and laughter with earnestness; they are suspicious and readily imagine that we disdain them.

To gain their perfect confidence and maintain it, it is well to let them come to our habitations, and not to let them leave without giving them eat and drink, and occasionally advance them some Powder, Lead, Tobacco. When they come in the evening, give them the liberty of laying beside the fire, then when we come again to them, they are even more friendly and hospitable.

Die 26. Frage.[2]

Ob sie das Gute belohnen, und das Böse straffen und wie?

R. **GUTES und Böses ist bey ihnen Natur und Gewohnheit, und hat keine gewisse Gräntzen** [auser in alleräusersten extremis] **als in extremis vitiis. Als Todtschlag, Zauberey und** [wie einige sagen] **Ehebruch,** [nach ihrer art] **die sind Capital, der König spricht die Sentenz.** [Doch können sie der Zeit erwarten, biss der Thäter in ihre Gelegenheit kommt, wo er sich nicht freiwillig einstellet. Die freundschafft dessen, der beleidiget, muss die Rache selbst, wo sie kann und die andere Parthey nicht fürchtet, ausführen es möchte denn seyn, dass der König Parthey nehme, welcher gleichwohl zu allem den *sentenz* spricht.] **Die Belohnung des Guten bestehet in dem Ruhm, und in einem nach ihrem Vermögen, gegenwärtigen Geschencke. Die Straffe bestehet bey dem Worte des Königs: Schlag ihn todt! worzu sich auch der Reus leicht bequemet, weil sie ihr Leben nicht hoch achten.**

Die 27. Frage.[3]

Von ihrem Regiment, ob sie einen König, oder viel Könige, und ob sie keinen andern Magistrat, und der König keine Ministros, sondern ganz alleine regiere?

R. **EINE Nation hat unterschiedliche Könige, und ein jeglicher König seine Vornehmsten, mit welchen er sich beratschlaget, es kan aber nicht leicht ein besserer Rath auskommen als des**

2 Question XXV in MSS.
3 Question XXVI in MSS.

The 26th Question.

Do they reward the good, and punish the evil, and how?

GOOD and evil are with them nature and usage, and have no certain boundaries except in the uttermost extremes, such as homicide, sorcery and some say adultery, which according to their manners are capital. Still they can await the time when the culprit returns to their locality. If he does not voluntarily surrender himself, the kinsmen of such as were injured must execute the revenge themselves, and must not fear the other party. It might be then that the chief takes a part, whose sentence would be binding upon all. The reward of the good consists in glory and in presents, according to their means and conditions.

The 27th Question.

Of their government. Have they one or many kings; have they any other magistates, and the king any ministers, or do they rule absolutely alone?

A NATION has different kings, and each king has his principals, with whom he takes counsel, but it is not easy to offer any better counsel than that of the king, as will be seen in the next question. Therefore, his word is as good as writ and deed. In public life king and subjects live almost without distinction.[25] Every one supports himself with hunting and fishing, etc.

Königs, wie aus folgendem wird zu sehen seyn. [wie aus fol-
gender *Question* wird zu ersehen seyn] Dahero ist sein
Wort so gut als Schrifft und That.   Im eusserlichen Thun aber
[bleiben] sind die Könige und Unterthanen fast einer wie der
andere, jeder nähret sich mit Jagen und Fischen rc.

Jeder König herrschet über ein gewisses Stück Landes, und
sind eitel Wahl-Königreiche, und muß ein König seyn der beste
Jäger, und der klügste Mann, so den besten Rath geben kan.
Des Königs Wort wird absolut vollzogen, doch ist er selbst der
erste der seinen Befehl thut.   Die Bedienung ist von denen andern
nicht unterschieden, und hat keinen Bedienten, ausser so er Feinde
hat, so stehen ihm seine Unterthanen zu Gebott, nnd bleiben in
seiner Hütten bey ihm.   Er conferirt mit den Klügsten vom
Volck, wann etwas wichtiges zu berathschlagen ist.   Wann der
Raum es zulässet, so sitzen sie rings umb das Feuer beym König.
Das Vermögen seiner Unterthanen ist so gut als das Seine, doch
fordert er nichts von ihnen, nnd des Königs Vermögen ist so gut,
als wäre es der Unterthanen.   Bißweilen bringen die Unterthanen etwas von ihrem Gelde, welches sie Wampon nennen, und
schwartz und weiß ist, wie eine Art von Schmeltz, oder langlechten
Glaß-Patterlen, wie geschnittener Heckerling, welches Geld auch
bey denen Europäern gilt, und Lagio darauf gegeben wird; sie
sagen aber nicht, wie sie es machen.

Wann sie ferne auf die Jagt gehen, oder in den Streit ziehen,
so stehet es denen Weibern frey welche mit gehen wollen, vor die
aber, so zu Hause bleiben, ordnet der König etliche Männer, daß
sie Wild vor die Hinterbliebene schiessen und sie versorgen.

In geringern *delictis* fangen sie an auch Geldstraffen zu gebrauchen.

Item wann ein Mann stirbet, der da schuldig ist, so bezahlet
die Freundschaft für ihn, weilen sie sich nicht wollen schimpffen
lassen.   Doch bitten sie umb Gedult.

Every king rules over a certain piece of territory, which is merely an elective kingdom, for a king must be the best hunter and the wisest man who can give the best advice. The king's word is absolutely obeyed, although he, himself, is the first to execute his own commands. His surroundings do not differ from the others, and he has no servants except when he has enemies, then all of his subjects are at his command, and remain in their huts near him. He confers with the wisest amongst his people when anything important is to be considered. Whenever the space permits they all sit around the fire with the king. The belongings of his subjects are as good as his, although he does not ask for them, and the king's property is the same as if it were that of the subjects. Sometimes the subjects bring him some of their money; this they call *wampum*. It is white and black, like a kind of enamel or lengthy glass pearling like cut chaff. This money also passes with the Europeans, and a premium is given for it; they will, however, not tell how they make it.

When they go upon an extended chase, or go upon the warpath, it is optional with the women if they want to go along. For such however as remain at home, the king orders divers men to remain and shoot game and provide for them.

For minor offences they also begin to impose fines of money.

Item, when a man dies, who is in debt, his kinsfolk pay for him, as they do not wish to be disgraced. Yet they pray for indulgence.

Die 28. Frage.[4]

Worinnen der König von andern unterschieden sey in Kleidung? Wohnung? eusserlicher Autorität ꝛc.

R. DAS vornehmste, welches den König von seinen Unterthanen unterscheidet, sind solche Qualitäten, die sie vor sonderlich achten als: Er muß seyn der Weiseste und Geschicklichste, starck, und der beste Jäger, daher ist ihr Königreich auch nicht erblich. Bißweilen ist sein, und seines Weibes Schmuck etwas bessers als der andern, und bestehet eigentlich darinnen, daß sie ihre Art Geldes [welches eine von uns unbekanten Dingen zusammengeschmolzene materie ist, die sie *wampon* nennen] wie Perlen nach der Schattierung zusammen scheuren, und entweder auf dem Kopffe, als eine Crone, oder auf die Brust, oder [wie nichts minder] umb die Haar-Zöpffe einflechten. [Das Vermögen der Unterthanen ist so gut, als wäre es des Königs, und seines so gut als ihres, wiewohl keiner von dem andern etwas begehret.] Des Königs Autorität gehet über alles, und sein Befehl wird ohne exception respectiret, doch ist er selbst der erste, der seinen Befehl ausrichtet.

Die 29. Frage.[5]

Wie denen Wilden einige Künste und Wissenschaften beyzubringen?

R. MAN muß ihnen dasjenige beybringen, worzu sie [solche müssen ihnen beygebracht werden, darzu sie nicht nur] ihrer Natur und Neigung nach incliniren, auch die Künste,

4 Question XXVII in MSS.
5 Question XXVIII in MSS.

CURIEUSE NACHRICHT VON PENNSYLVANIA.

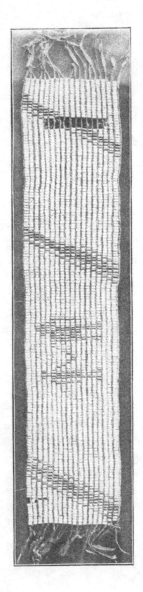

NOT SWORN TO AND NEVER BROKEN
THE
BELT OF WAMPUM
GIVEN TO WILLIAM PENN BY THE LENI LENAPE SACHEMS AT THE ELM TREE TREATY, SHACKAMAXON, IN 1682.
PRESENTED BY GRANVILLE JOHN PENN TO THE HISTORICAL SOCIETY OF PENNSYLVANIA.

The 28th Question.

Wherein the King differs from the others in dress,
habitation, outward authority, etc.

THE superiority in which the king differs from his
subjects are such qualities as they specially ad-
mire. Thus he must be the wisest among them, as well
as the bravest, most expert and powerful hunter. Therefore, the king is wealthy and the office is not inheritable.
Occasionally his and his wives' adornments are somewhat
better than the others, and represent his wealth. They
have a kind of money, which is composed of materials
unknown to us and fused together; this they call *wampum*,[27] and string like pearls according to the shading. It
is worn either upon the head as a crown, or upon the
chest, for nothing more or less than to braid in their queus.[28]
The belongings of the subject are the same as if they were
the king's, and his as well as theirs, although no one asks
anything from another. His authority is absolute over all,
and his commands are respected without exception. Yet
he is among the first to execute his own commands.

The 29th Question.

How to introduce some of the arts and sciences
among the savages.

SUCH only must be communicated to them toward
which they are inclined by their nature and habits,
and such as are not prejudicial to the Europeans. Among

die denen Europäern nit præjudicirlich sind, als [also untern andern die vornehmsten sind:] Mahlerey, [und] Music, [sondern auch dadurch man desto naher zu dem rechten Zweck bey ihnen gelangen und zum wenigsten etliche der ihrigen zu einer andern Sprache in lesen und schreiben gewohnen könne] und Schreiberey, wordurch man sie am leichtesten zu einer andern Sprache gewöhnen kan. Wo benebens man sie durch allerhand offtmahls wiederholte Lockung, und freundliche Darreichung der Liebe, an sich ziehen muß, doch sie nicht allzu fest halten, daß sie suspiciren können, ob wolte man sie in ihrer Freyheit einschräncken, vielmehro ihren Gemüthern zuvor kommen, ehe [und bevor] sie eines Dinges müde werden. Darzu aber werden Leute erfordert, die sonst nichts anders zu thun haben.

Die 30. Frage.[6]

Wie ihnen etwa einige Principia generalia Religionis beyzubringen?

R. WANN man nur erst einige derselben auf schon angeregte gute Gründe gebracht hat, daß sie die Englische oder Teutsche Sprache lernen verstehen, dann kann man sie auf die Erkanntnuß Gottes, nach den Wercken der ersten Schöpffung führen, und sie darinnen bey täglichen Umbgang bekräfftigen, biß GOtt [weiter gelegenheit ihnen ein mehres anzuvertrauen zeiget] sie weiters erleuchtet.

[6] Question XXIX in MSS.

others the principal ones are music and painting; we should seek thereby to come closer with them toward our true object, and induce a few at least to learn to read and write another language. Moreover, we should seek to draw them to us by all kinds of repeated friendly allurement and offerings of love; being careful not to hold them so fast as to arouse their suspicion, as if we wanted to curtail their liberty, but rather to anticipate their wishes, before they tire of anything. For this purpose persons will be needed who have naught else to do.

The 30th Question.

How to introduce among them some of the general principles of religion.[29]

IF some of them could only have been brought up on the already mentioned lines, so that they understood the English or German tongue, then we could lead them to a knowledge of God through the story of the first creation, and then by daily intercourse strengthen them, until God grants us further opportunity to show them greater confidence.

Die 31. Frage.[7]

Wie man ihnen realiter das rechtschaffene Wesen eines
Christen vor Augen stellen könne, daß ihnen das Licht
in die Augen leuchte, und einige Funcken in
ihrem Gemüth erwecke.

R. WANN die vorhergehende [XXVIII und XXIX][8] Fragen
wohl practicirt worden sind, alsdann wird man erst
recht absehen, wie [man diese Frage beantworten soll] ferner
zu procediren.

Die 32. Frage.[9]

Wie man meinet, daß die Wilden in Americam kommen
und zwar die unterschiedliche Nationes?

R. HJervon sind unterschiedliche Meinungen. [welche denen
studio geographico geübten besser bekant sind als
mir] Bey uns hält man darfür, daß die Sudische Indianer von
Africa herüber kommen. Die Nordischen von denen Insulis
Azoribus oder Flandrischen Insuln. Die alten Grallier oder
Britannier wollen [glaubwürdig] beweisen, daß vor etwan mehr
als 1000. Jahren ein [einer oder zwey von ihren damaligen
König söhnen] Paar ihrer Königs-Söhnen (nachdem ihre
Königliche Familia fast groß worden) [umb neues Land,
welches man nahe bey zu finden vermeinet,] sich mit einigen
ihren Unterthanen zur See begeben, und [endlich] in Arme-
niam Septentrionalem [angekommen sei] geschiffet, dahero
bey denen Indianern noch eine sonderbahre Nation befindlich,

[7] Question XXX in MSS.
[8] Alludes to questions in original MSS.
[9] Question XXXI in MSS.

The 31st Question.

How one could properly place before them the true,
righteous nature of a christian, so that the light
would shine into their eyes, and divers
sparks awaken their nature.

AFTER the 29th and 30th questions have been well
practiced, then we shall readily see how this
question should be answered.

The 32nd Question.

How it is supposed that the savages came to America
and in particular the different nations.

HEREUPON there are different opinions, which are
known better to such as are versed in geographical
studies than to me.[30] With us, we hold that the southern
Indians[31] came over from Africa, the Northern Indians
from the Azores, or Flemish Islands.[32] The ancient Gauls
or Britons claim to have trustworthy proof that more than
one thousand years ago one or two sons of the then reign-
ing king (after the royal family had grown up) with a
number of their subjects set out to sea, to discover new
lands, which it was thought would be found nearby.
Eventually they reached North America.[33] This appears
all the more probable, as there is said to have been found

126 **Curieuse Nachricht von Pennsylvania.**

welche die alte Grallische und Britannische Sprache noch reden
soll. [welches dahero fast glaubwürdig ist, weil sich eine
Nation der Indianer findet welche die alte Gallische oder
Britische Sprache auf eine gebrochene doch kentliche
weise reden soll. Von welcher sache mir bey meiner
wiederkunfft schriftliche zeugnisse und alte *monumenta*
aufzuweisen versprochen worden.]

Die 33. Frage.[10]

**Wie denen Wilden die Teutsche oder Englische Sprache
beyzubringen?**

R. [**DIESE Frage**] **Ist bereits** [Question XXVIII][11] **oben
beantwortet, und könnte** [dieses wäre noch hinzuzu-
fügen dass] **auch durch fromme Handels-Leute** [welche der
wilden sprache erst wohl gelernet ein grosser Beytrag
geshehen könte, wann man nur die rechte stange zu halten
wüste] **ein grosses in freundlicher Conversation beygetragen
werden, doch müste es durch keine andere geschehen, als nur durch
die jenigen, welche alleine zur Ehre Gottes an ihnen etwas ten-
tiren wollen.**

Die 34. Frage.[12]

Ob nicht bey ihren Kindern solches angehn?

R. **DIE Kinder sind niemahls ohne die Eltern, noch die
Eltern ohne die Kinder, weilen sie eine rechte Affen-
Liebe zusammen haben:** [deswegen man diesen Vortheil an

[10] Question XXXII in MSS.
[11] Question XXVIII in MSS.
[12] Question XXXIII in MSS.

a tribe of Indians, who still speak the Gallic or British tongue in a broken yet recognizable way. In regard to this matter, written proof and old documents are promised me upon my return.[34]

The 33rd Question.

How to introduce the German or English tongue among the savages.

THIS question has already been answered in Question 29. We may add, however, that perhaps, by aid of pious tradespeople, who have learned the language of the savage, great knowledge might be gained how to bridle them.[35] However, this must and can be done by none save such as are willing to strive somewhat for God's glory.

The 34th Question.

Would such be possible with their children?

THE children are never away from their parents, nor the parents without their children, as they have a foolish fondness for their children.[36] Therefore, to gain

ihnen zu haben eine *Colonie* in der nähe ihrer meisten Heymath und *cours* anlegen müsste, so könte man jung und alt immer *iteratis vicibus* an sich locken.] **Müste man also eine Coloniam näher zu ihnen bauen, daß man näher bey ihnen wäre, und Junge und Alte** per quotidianam consuetudinem iteratis vicibus **an sich ziehen könte.**

Die 35. Frage.[13]

Ob nicht fromme Teutsche dort ihre Kinder mit Freundlichkeit an sich halten, und sie dergestalt zur Sprache anleiten können.

R. **DIESES wäre mehr** [vor ein wunder göttlicher schickung zu achten] **als eine Wunderschickung Gottes, dann** [vor eine zulässliche möglichkeit ihrer natur und art] **es ihrer Natur und Art halber unmöglich.**

Die 36. Frage.[14]

Ob ihnen nicht auf solche Weise gute Principia Timoris Dei **beyzubringen, darauf noch ferner nach und nach Gutes zu erbauen?**

R. **DIESE Frage ist aus vorhergehenden allschon beantwortet** [welchem ich über das *Exempel* der *Presbyterianer* in *New England* noch dieses beyfüge: Es wohnt ein

---

[13] Question XXXIV in MSS.
[14] Question XXXV in MSS.

any advantage a colony would have to be located near their most populous places ; then both young and old might be *iteratis vicibus*, tempted to come to us.

The 35th Question.

Whether devout Germans there could by friendliness attach their children unto them, and in such manner induce them to learn the language?

THAT, according to their nature and habits, would be more of a miracle of Divine dispensation than an admissible possibility.

The 36th Question.

Whether in this manner good *principia timoris Dei* might not be impressed upon them, whereupon to gradually build good results?

THIS refers to that which has preceded, to which I will add the following, against the example set by the Presbyterians in New England. There lives in East

Bauer aus Holstein bürtig in *Ost Jersey*, welcher nachdem
re der Indianischen sprache wohl kundig, dieselben ohne
Rede zum guten anweiset und weil sie durch seine Liebe
und freywillige Aufnahme eine sehr gute *persuasion* von
ihm haben, so sind viele ihm gehorsam und wann er sie
um des bösen halber gegenwärtig bestrafet, thun sie es
hernach nicht mehr, welches ich glaubwürdig gehöret.]
die wilden laſſen ſich nicht ſo tieff in Conversation ein, indeme
ſie die Sprachen nicht verſtehen.

Die 37. Frage.[15]

Ob nicht auf dieſe Weiſe durch die Kinder auch die Alten zu gewinnen?

R. JST auch in beeden vorhergehenden beantwortet. [Alt
und jung, jung und Alt, wie es die Göttliche *Providenz* in ihrer ewigen Erbarmung ausweisen wird das
ist gewiss; wo ernstlich einige zu solchen umständen gebracht dann sollen sie selbst am geschicktesten seyn,
Gottes werk unter ihrer Nation zu würcken, und von daher
würde man auch eine Gelegenheit haben, andern Nationen
beyzukommen.

15 Question XXXVI in MSS.

Jersey a farmer born in Holstein, who, after becoming
well versed in the Indian tongue, directs them without
many words to that which is good; and as they have a
very good opinion of him through his love and voluntary
welcome, many obey him, and when he chides them for
transgressions or evildoing, they do not repeat it hereafter.
All of which I have learned from trustworthy sources.
The savages do not enter deeply into conversation as they
do not understand the language.

The 37th Question.

Could we not in this manner reach the Elders through the children?

HAS been answered in the two preceding ones. Old
and young — young and old — just as divine providence in its everlasting mercy will demonstrate. Certain
it is, where a few firstlings can be brought to such conditions, then they would be best qualified to spread the word
of God among their nation, whereby we should have an
opportunity to introduce it to other nations.

Die 38. Frage.[16]

Wie die Wilden jetzt ihren Cultum halten, was sie an= beten, wie sie opffern?

R. **PATER** Hennepius hat hiervon geschrieben, [Davon kan unter *Pater Hennepius* Beschreibung nachgelesen werden] aber andere Scriptores thun denen Indianern zu viel, wann sie vorgeben, als ob sie manifeste den Teuffel anbeteten, da sie doch keine Bilder noch Götzen leiden. [noch haben] Item als ob [dass] sie stets Menschen frässen, [welches man so nimmt, als ob sie allezeit menschen ässen so viel sie der- selben bekämen, da doch dieses nur ein Krieges recht bey ihnen, indem sie glauben, dass man sich an seinen Fein- den nicht rächen könne, so sey denn, dass man sein Fleisch frässe, deswegen sie aus allen in Streit gefangenen Toden 3 von den fettesten und fleischigsten zum Dankopfer vor dem Sieg und sich selbst zur *satisfaction* genommener *revanche* braten und essen] da es doch nur nach erobertem Kriege an ihren Feinden zu einer Rache geschiehet, de quo postea. Sonsten ist ihr Cultus ein grober heydnischer Manichæismus: Von einem guten und bösen GOtt. Von einem warmen und kalten Lande, da der Mensch nach seinen guten oder bösen Meriten hinwandere, wann er nicht mehr hier sey.

[16] Question XXXVII in MSS.

The 38th Question.

How the savages now keep their cult, what they worship, and as to their sacrificial rite.

WHEREOF we may read among other descriptions that of *Pater Hennesius.*[37] However, writers and readers charge them with too much, when they intimate that the Indians manifestly worship the devil, as they neither have nor tolerate any idols or pictures. Item, that they are Cannibals, which is taken as if they ate human beings at all times or as often as they could get them. This is merely done as a martial duty,[38] with them, as they believe that one cannot revenge himself completely upon his enemies unless their flesh be eaten. Therefore they always sacrifice two or three of their fattest and plumpest prisoners as a thankoffering for their victory; and, for their own self-satisfaction in having gained their revenge, roast and eat them. Otherwise their cult is a coarse heathenish *Manichæism* of a good and evil deity and of a warm and cold country, whereto the being wanders according to his good or bad merits, when he is here no longer.

Die 39. Frage. [17]

Wie sie vorhin gelebet, ehe die Europäer hinein kommen?

R. EBEN so wie nun, nur daß ihrer eine grössere Menge ge=
wesen, und ihres Gottesdienstes viel eifferiger abgewar=
tet [also nun] dahero die Verständigste unter ihnen diese Klage
führen: Unsere Generation lebet nicht mehr so gut, als unsere
Vorfahren.

Die 40. Frage. [18]

Was sie nun von denen Europäern angenommen?

R. GUTES und Böses. Eine mehrere Leutseligkeit, und
Begierde allerhand Neues zu sehen, und dasselbige nach=
zumachen. [Einige] Nach unserer Art mit Büchsen zu schiessen,
[werk machen um] den Leib zu bedecken, [allerhand unter-
schied von Dingen, von Kaufmannswaaren und Geld etc.]
Geldzehlen, Saltzessen, Brandwein= und Bier trincken, Gewürtz=
essen, und Schweinefleisch essen, [der gleichen sie vorhero nicht
gehabt] dahero sie unsern Krankheiten unterworfen ꝛc. [und
sterben] auch darneben nicht mehr so fruchtbar sind, als sie vor=
hero waren. Welches aller Nationen billich ein nachdenkliches
[nachdrückliches] Nota Bene seyn solte, daß sie nicht leicht
ihre Diät [in einem frembden Lande fahren lassen] fahren
lassen, und sich an die Art frembder Ankömlinge gewöhnen solten.

[17] Question XXXVIII in MSS.
[18] Question XXXIX in MSS.

The 39th Question.

How they lived prior to the advent of the Europeans.

———

JUST the same as now, only that their numbers were much greater, and they were much more zealous in their worship than now. Consequently the wise ones among them have the same plaint that one now hears everywhere: "That our generation does not live as well as our ancestors."

———

The 40th Question.

What they have adopted from the Europeans.

———

GOOD and evil: A more humane disposition to see all sorts and manners of what is new, and to imitate the same. Thus some want to shoot with the rifle according to our manner; others make cloth [39] to cover their bodies; they learn all kinds of distinctions in merchandize, money, etc., the eating of salt; the drinking of brandy and beer; the eating of spices, also pork and the like, which they never had before. By all these things they were subjected to our diseases and death; further they are likewise not nearly so prolific as they were formerly, which should be a fair and forcible warning [40] to all people that they should not readily abandon their own diet in a foreign land, and adopt that of strange nations.

Die 41. Frage.[19]
Von der Wilden ihren Curen und Kranckheiten?

1. R. WAnn sie Fieberische Anstösse haben, oder sich nicht wohl befinden, so kochen sie schwarze Nuß-Rinden in Wasser, und trincken es in grosser Menge, binden sich umb den Leib und Kopff mit Stricken aus wilden Hanff.

2. Sie schwitzen auf folgende Art: Sie machen eine niedrige Hütte, so hoch daß sie nur darinnen sitzen können, bedecken sie biß auf die Erde mit Baum-Rinden und mit Fellen, und machen heraussen vor der Hütten etliche glüende Steine, die tragen sie in ein Loch in der Hütten, setzen sich darüber, und schwitzen so violent und starck, daß die Erde unter ihnen naß wird, so unmöglich von einem Europäer ausgestanden werden kan. Wann sie nun genug geschwitzet, so lauffen sie heraus nnd springen in einen kalten Bach, damit sind sie curirt.

3. Sie haben eine Wurtzel, so die Schlangen vertreibet, welche sie an das Bein binden, und lauffen damit durch den Wald, und nehmen keinen Schaden von Schlangen. Haben sie aber diese Wurtzel nicht, und werden von Schlangen gebissen, so schneiden sie gleich den Biß aus dem Fleisch.

4. Geschwulsten, Flüsse, Verrenckungen der Glieder zu curiren, da lassen sie es bluten, und schneiden mit einem scharffen Stein, als ein Flintenstein die Haut durch, ohne daß sie eine Ader verletzen, welches sie wohl zu unterscheiden wissen, und halten das Glied bey das Feuer, und nehmen ein Holtz, schaben damit das Blut ab, daß es nicht gerinnen kan, biß es ausgeblutet hat, dann waschen sie die Wunden mit Wasser ab, und haben gewisse Wurtzeln, diese quetschen sie zwischen zwey Steine, und legen sie mit wenigen grünen Blättern über, das heylet in einer Nacht.

[19] Not among the original Questions.

The 41st Question.

(The following eight questions do not appear in the
original MSS.)

Concerning the diseases and cures of the Savages.

1. When they have feverish attacks, or do not feel well,
they boil the black hulls of nuts[41] in water and drink large
quantities of it, and bind themselves about the abdomen
and head with bands of wild hemp.

2. They sweat themselves in the following manner, they
build a low hut, just high enough to permit them to sit
upright, they cover it down to the ground with bark and
skins, they then heat some stones outside to a red heat,
and place them in a hole within the hut, and then sit over
them causing them to sweat so powerful and violently as to
wet the earth beneath them, which would be impossible
for any European to endure. When they have sweated
sufficiently, they run out and plunge into a cold stream.[42]
Then they are cured.

3. They have a root which drives away the snakes, this
they bind about their legs, and run through the woods,
and receive no injury from the snakes. However, if they
have none of this root, and are bitten by the snakes, they
immediately cut the bite out of the flesh.

4. To cure swellings, humors or sprains (dislocations)
of the limbs they let them bleed and cut with a sharp stone,
generally a piece of flint, through the skin, without injur-
ing any artery, which they well know how to distinguish,
they then hold the member near the fire, and with a piece
of wood scrape off the blood that it cannot coagulate, until
it has ceased bleeding, then they wash the wound, with
water, and have certain roots which they bruise between

5. Wann sie Schiffern in die Füß getretten haben, so schneiden sie es mit einem Messer rein aus, und schmieren von Schlangen=Fett die Wunden, und heilens wieder.

6. Vor innerliche Zustände essen sie die kleine Gedärme so mit Fett bewachsen, von denen jungen Thieren.

Die 42. Frage.

Was die Wilden für Krieg führen?

R. DIE Wilden haben selten Friede, und werden von ihren eigenen Nationen angefochten, und können die Ursachen von geringer Feindschafft hergenommen werden, oder auch, wann sie einander in das Gebiethe jagen.

Ihr Fechten geschicht erstlich in einzelen Partheyen, da Mann und Mann oder 2. 3. mit einander schlagen, und solches mit Bogen, Aexten, Röhren, Flinten, und thun solches gemeiniglich auf der Jagt, da nehmen sie einander gefangen, und verkauffen die Gefangene. Wann sich aber die Widerwärtige sammeln, und sie eine Schlacht Ordnung machen, So tretten sie in einen Creiß, daß der Feind auf allen Seiten ihre Angesichter sehen kan, und wann einer todt geschossen wird, oder blessirt, so stossen sie solchen in den Creiß hinein, und machen den Craiß enger. Wann sie Gefangene bekomen, so verkauffen sie ein Stück 2. 3. der Fettesten, und braten sie, und essen sie, weilen alle Südliche Indiauer glauben, da man sich an seinem Feinde nicht besser rächen könne, es sey dann daß man sein Fleisch fresse, zumahl sie auch das Fleisch ihres gleichen höher achten als alles Wildpret, aus der Ursachen, daß die Ihrige nicht saltzigt, sondern gantz süsse sind, da hingegen die Engelländer und Franzosen sehr saltzig und ungeschmack wären.

two stones, and lay upon it with some green leaves, this heals in a single night.

5. When they run any splints into their feet, they cut the wound out clean with a knife, and smear snake fat in the wound, then it heals.

6. For internal conditions, they eat the small sebaceous intestines of young animals.

The 42nd Question.

The warfare of the Savages.

THE savages are seldom at peace, and are attacked by their own kind, the causes may arise from trifling enmities or when they trespass in the chase upon each others territory.

Their fighting in the first instance consist of small parties, where man fights with man, or two or three battle with one another, this they do with bows, axes, guns and rifles, and it generally occurs when they are out upon the chase, they also make captives and sell the prisoners. When, however, their opponents gather, and they form an order of battle, they arrange themselves in a circle, so that upon all sides their faces are turned toward the enemy and when one is shot dead or wounded, they draw within the circle, thus making it smaller. When they take any prisoners, they sell two or three of the fattest to be roasted and eaten, as all Southern Indians believe that one can have no greater revenge upon their enemies, than by eating their flesh, at the same time they regard the flesh of the natives better than all venison, for the reason that the savage meat is not salty but good and sweet, while upon the other hand, that of the Englishman and French is very salty and tasteless.[43]

Sie bedienen sich allerhand Kriegsliste, ihre Feinde zu über=
winden, so wohl einzele, als mit gantzen Partheyen. Einzele,
daß sie observiren die Weege der Partheyen, weil sie solches ge=
nau observiren können aus den Sträuchen und Graß, aus wel=
chem sie gewiß abnehmen können, ob ein Mann oder Frau, ein
Kind, ein Europäer oder Wilder darüber gangen.

Item steigen sie in der Nacht auf die hohen Berge, und sehen
hier und dar hin, wo sie Feuer und Holtz gewahr werden, darnach
gehen sie zu, und kommen an der andern Seiten vom Feuer ihnen
auf den Leib, und tödten oder schiessen sie wann sie schlaffen (gegen
die Partheyen gebrauchen sie den Vorthel, daß sie sie in die Enge
treiben, damit sie sie können gefangen nehmen. Und weilen die
Franzosen etliche bekehret haben, die nun den Sonntag feyren, so
kommen die andern, so keinen Sonntag feyern, und überfallen sie.

Die 43. Frage.

Von der Wilden ihren eigentlichen Haußhalten?

R. JHRE Wohnung ist an keinem beständigen Orte, darumb
auch ihre Haußhaltung veränderlich, daß Hauß ist biß=
weilen an einem alten liegenden Baum gemacht, wann es aber
ein gantzes ist, so stehet es frey, ist aber nur Manns hoch, in der
Mitten oben ist es offen, daß der Rauch des Feuers, so Mitten
in der Hütten ist, hinaus ziehen kan. Die Hütten ist mit Rin=
den von Bäumen zugedeckt, und rings herum mit dergleichen ver=
wahret, inwendig haben sie es mit Stroh, oder mit langem Grase
umbsetzet, etliche machen Tapezereyen von gefärbtem Stroh, und
zieren ihr Hauß, welches in ihrer Sprach Wickwam heisset.

Im fall daß sie ausserhalb des Hauses ergriffen werden von
einem Regen, nehmen sie eine bey sich habende Decke, spannen sie

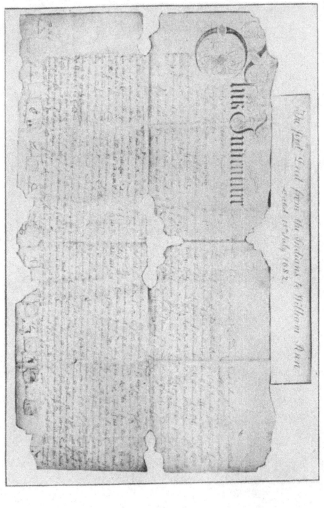

INDIAN DEED.

They use all kinds of stratagem to overcome their enemies, whether single or in parties. Singly, they examine
the tracks of parties and by the accurate observation of
the bushes and grass, can tell positively whether it was a
man, woman or child, European or Savage had passed
over the ground. Likewise, they climb high mountains
at night, and spy about, here and there, to catch sight of
any fire in the woods. Then they approach from the
other side of the fire, attack, and kill or shoot them, while
they are asleep. Against parties they take advantage to
hem them in, so that they may capture them. And now
as the French have converted divers of them, who now
keep the Sabbath, such as do not keep the Sabbath sur-
prise and attack them upon that day.

The 43d Question.

Of the domestic life of the savages.

THEIR dwellings are in no settled place and their
housekeeping is variable. It is occasionally made
against an old fallen tree, but when it is a complete one,
it stands clear, but is only the height of a man. It is open
in the middle, so that the smoke of the fire, which is in the
center of the hut, may escape. The huts are covered with
the bark of trees and are thus protected, the interior is
lined with straw or long grasses, some weave mats out of
colored straw to ornament their huts, which in their language they call a wickwam. If they are overtaken by a
rain when away from home, they take a mat, which they
carry, and stretch it out like a roof, and sit under it, or

aus wie ein Dach, und setzen sich darunter, oder machen ein groß
Feuer, und werffen allerhand faul Holtz darauf, daß es viel Rauch
gibt, legen sich an dieselbige Seiten, da der Wind den Rauch
hinwehet, so zertheilet der Rauch den Regen, und das, was noch
auf sie fällt, ist durch den Rauch uud die Glut warm worden.
    In ihrer Hütten sitzen sie auf Büscheln Graß oder Hirschfellen.
Und des Nachts decken sie sich mit dergleichen, oder mit einem
Bärenfell, oder mit einer Wollene Decke, oder mit einer Decke
von Calcunen=Federn sehr künstlich zusammen gewürcket, und
nehmen die kleinsten Kinder eins vor sich an Leib, und eins an
den Rücken.

Die 44. Frage.
Von der Wilden ihrem Haußrathe.

R. JHR Haußrath bestehet von einem Stück von einem abge=
    hauenen Baume, oder auch der noch mit der Wurtzel im
Grunde fest stehet, in den brennen sie in der Mitten mit Schwam=
men ein Loch, als eine tieffe Schüssel oder Mörsner hinein, darin=
nen stossen sie ihr Indianisch Korn, darvon sie Brod backen,
welches sie Ponn nennen, und auch Suppen davon kochen, welche
sie Sapan nennen. Das Korn besprengen sie mit heissem Wasser,
und stampffen es, daß die Schaale herab gehet, und stoffen es
klein, saigen das Kleinste durch ein Strohernes Körbgen, und
formiren Brod als grosse Ziegen=Käse daraus, stecken sie in die
heisse Aschen, und scharren die Kohlen darüber, und backen es
also, wann es gar ist, waschen sie das Brod mit Wasser ab, sie
mengen auch bißweilein rothe, oder andere Farb Bohnen unter
das Brod, welches dann siehet als ob Rosinen darein gebacken
wären. Nechst diesem haben sie einen Kessel, darinn kochen sie
ihr Fleisch von Hirschen, das Fleisch aber waschen sie nicht, und

they make a large fire and throw all kinds of decayed wood upon it, that it makes much smoke, and lay themselves upon that side, toward which the wind drives the smoke, so that smoke disperses the rain, and that which falls upon them has been warmed by the smoke and burning embers.

In their huts they sit upon tussocks of grass or deerskins, and at night cover themselves with them, or with a bear skin, or with a woolen blanket, or with a cover of feathers very artistically woven together, then they put the smallest child in front of them and one at the back.

The 44th Question.

Of the savages' Household utensils.

Their household utensils consist of a piece of a hewn tree, or one which still stands fast with its roots in the ground. In the middle of this they burn a hole with fungus, like a deep bowl or mortar. In this they pound their Indian corn, whereof they make bread, which they call *Ponn*. They also make a soup of it which they call *Sapan*. They sprinkle the corn with hot water, and stamp it to loosen the hulls; then they pound it fine, sift the finest through a straw basket, and make loaves like large goat's milk cheeses. Then they place them in hot ashes and rake the coals over them, and so bake them. When they are sufficiently baked they wash the loaves off with water. Occasionally they also mix red or other colored beans among the bread, which then looks as though raisins were baked in it. —Besides this they have a kettle, wherein they cook their deer meat, which they do

vermeinen, es entgehe ihnen die Krafft, sie schaumen es auch nicht
ab, was aber überkocht, das lassen sie gehen.   Das blutige Fleisch
lieben sie, und halten es für gesund, denn kochen sie Bohnen oder
gestossen Korn in der Fleisch=Brühe, sie kochen auch Schildkroten
ohne Kessel unter den Kohlen in ihrer eigenen Schalen, zu denen
Vögeln nehmen sie sich nicht der Zeit wann sie klein sind, so bren=
nen sie die Federn auf dem Feuer ab.   Von Calcunen aber, ge=
brauchen sie die Federn zum Decken zu würcken.   Sie essen auch
Füchse, fette Hunde, Bisam=Katzen, Biber, Eichhörner und
Habichte.   Zum braten haben sie nichts nöthig als einen Pfahl,
den machen sie uff beeden Seiten spitzig, und stecken ihn mit der
einen Spitzen in den Grund, uff der andern Seiten stecken sie daß
Fleisch diinn geschnitten daran, und kehren es zu Zeiten umb.

Der übrige Haußrath ist ein Kalibas, oder ausgehohlter Kür=
bis zum Trinckgeschirr, Höltzerne Löffel, die sie selbst nach ihrem
Munde machen, in deren Ermanglung gebrauchen sie Muscheln
und Austern=Schalen.   Ihre Höltzerne Schüsseln werden von
Knotten der Bäume gemacht, oder von harten Kürbis=Rinden.
Mancher hat 2. oder 3. Säcke von wildem Hanff gemacht, und
durch die gefärbte Schattirung von braun, roth, und weiß artig
zusammen gesetzt, kleinere machen sie von dem Stroh des Indiani=
schen Korns, darinn tragen sie ihren Haußrath mit sich nebst einem
kleinen Beilgen, so sie Domehicken nennen, welche sie nun von
denen Europäern bekommen, sonsten haben sie harte Steine an
statt dessen gebrauchet, von welchen Steinen sie auch ihre Beile
machen, ist ein brauner Stein als ein Blut=Stein, welchen sie
durch viel Klopffen scharpff und spitzig machen.

Ihre Scheuren machen sie in die Erde, graben ein Loch Manns=
tieff, als ein Brunnen, sezens es mit langem Graße aus, und da
thun sie ihr Indianisch Korn, Kürbis und andere Sachen hinein.
Die Hunde und Schweine können sie gewöhnen, daß sie nie von
ihrem Gesichte kommen, sondern stets ihrer Stimme folgen, des
Nachts legen sie die Schweine an Stricke an, und wann sie fett

not wash, as they think it would take out the strength, nor do they skim it, but what runs over they let go. They like their meat bloody, and regard it as healthy. Then they cook beans or crushed corn in the meat broth. They also cook tortoises without any pot, under the coals in their own shells. As to birds they devote but little time; if small, they simply singe off the feathers with fire; of the wild turkeys, however, they use the feathers to work into covers. They also eat foxes, fat dogs, civit cats, beavers, squirrels and hawks. For roasting they need nothing but a stake—this they point at both ends. One end they stick into the ground, upon the other they stick the meat cut thin, and turn it at times.

The rest of their furniture consists of a calabash, or a hollowed out pumpkin for a drinking vessel, wooden spoons, which they make to suit their mouth, or else they use mussel or oyster shells. Their wooden bowls are made of the knots of trees or of hard pumpkin rind. Many a one has two or three sacks made of wild hemp, which by the dyed shading of brown, red and white, is artistically put together. Smaller ones they make of the straw of the Indian corn, in which they carry their household utensils and a little hatchet, which they call *Domehicken* [44] and now get from the Europeans. Formerly they used hard stones instead. The stone from which they make their axes, is a brown stone like blood, [45] which they sharpen and point by many blows.

Their granaries, they build in earth, they dig a hole, the depth of a man, like a well, and line it with long grasses, and then put in their Indian corn, pumpkins, and other things. [46] They train their dogs and swine so as not to leave their sight, also always to follow their voice. At night they secure the swine with ropes, and when they are

geworden sind, verkauffen sie solche den Europäern umb Brante=
wein, weilen sie das Schweinen=Fleisch nicht hoch æstimiren.

Die 45. Frage.

Von denen Thieren, so in Pensylvania zu befinden?

R. DA sind Bären, Pantherthier, Hirschen, welche nicht so
groß wie in Europa, jedoch fetter und von besserm Ge=
schmack, weisse Rehe und Weiter ins Holtz hinein Sudwestwerts
gibt es wilde Ochsen und wilde Kühe, Luxen, und wilde Katzen,
welche dem grossen Wild grossen Schaden thun, springen von
Bäumen dem Viehe auf den Rucken. Zweyerley Wölffe, schwarze
und graue, unter denen die schwarzen am ärgsten, sie fallen aber
keinen Menschen an. Füchse, Racunen, Bisam=Katzen, Hasen,
Aichhörner schwartz und grau sehr groß und sehr fett, auch eine
Art von Eichhörnern, welche fliegen können, auch rothe Mäuse
wie die Haselmäuse.

Die 46. Frage.

Was gibt es dann für Wasser=Thiere?

R. BIBER die Menge, bleiben unter dem Wasser allezeit
trucken, welches wegen Glatte der Haare nicht daran
hafftet, sie fressen Fische, und fangen die Endten. Fisch=Otter,
Mincken, diese riechen wie die Marten. Museus=Ratten, deren
Felle man zu denen Kleidern legt, so kommt keine Motten darein.
Schildkroten groß und kleine, welche im Winter in den Marast
kriechen.
Meerschweine, Störs, Springers, Elffster oder Schattfisch,
welche im Früh=Jahr sehr häufig gefangen und eingesaltzen wer=

fattened they sell them to the Europeans for rum, as they do not esteem pork highly.

The 45th Question.

Of the animals to be found in Pennsylvania.

THERE are bears, panthers, deers, which are not so large as in Europe, though fatter and of a better taste, white does and elks.

Further in the forest towards the southwest there are wild oxen and wild cows, lynx and wild cats, which do great damage to the larger game, as they spring from the trees upon the backs of the animals. Two kinds of wolves, black and grey, of these the black ones are the worst, but they do not attack people. Foxes, racoons, skunks, hares, squirrels, black and grey, very large and fat, also a sort of flying squirrels and red mice like unto the common dormouse.

The 46th Question.

What kind of aquatic animals are there?

BEAVER in quantity, they remain dry under water all the time, which does not adhere to the hair on account of its sleekness, they eat fish and catch the ducks. Fish otters, minks, which smell like martens. Muskrats, whose skins when laid among clothing, are a sure preventative against moths. Turtles great and small which creep into the mud during the winter. Porpoises, sturgeon, springers (salmon?). Shad fish which are caught in great

deu, sind ungemein fett, und wie Laxe, nur daß sie einige kleine Gräten im Fleisch haben. Zwölffer oder Rock, und Dromfisch. Item Suckers vom Saugen, weil sie das Grüne im Wasser saugen, Börsing zweyerley, Sonnenfisch, welche als Silber und Gold glänzen, Forellen, Hechte, bleiben in diesem Lande gantz klein, weilen sie keine marastige Ufer haben. Krebse auch kleine wegen mangelns marastigen Ufern. Aalen, Neunaugen und allerhand Seefische.

Die 47. Frage.

Was gibt es dann für schädliche Thier im Wasser?

R. Allerhand Art Schlangen, die durchs Wasser schwimmen können, denen die Schildkrotten, nachstellen, und solche, wo sie ihrer mächtig werden können, fressen. Dieser Schlangen Stich ist nicht tödtlich, sondern gehet mit einer schnellen Schwellung wiederum vorbey.

Auf dem Lande gibt es Rattel-Schlangen, welche im zweiten Jahre Ratteln kriegen, und so viel Jahre sie älter werden, so viel Ratteln mehr, diese haben Zähne, durch welche sie den Gifft insinuiren. Sie vermehren sich durch Eyerlegen, darbey doch die Sonne das beste thun muß, ihre Nahrung sind Frosche, Kröten, Wiesel, wann ihren kleinen Jungen ein Thier oder Mensche zu nahe kommt, so kriechen sie wieder in die Mutter hinein. Nechst diesen sind Vipern grau von Coleur wie Schiffer, wann sie im Felde liegen, haben sie den Kopff in die Erde verborgen, und wann man sie irritiret, geben sie einen Laut von sich, wie eine böse Katze. Nattern sind kleine geschwinde und röthliche Schlangen, ihr Bauch siehet Saffrangelb, und also ein überaus vergifftetes Thier. Auch gibt es dreyerley Art Frösche. 1. eine Mittelgattung, wie die unserige in Teutschland. 2. eine kleinere

numbers in spring and salted down, they are exceedingly fat, just like salmon, only that they have small bones in the flesh, rock and drum fish. Likewise suckers, from sucking as they suck the greens in the water, perch two kinds, sunfish, which shine like silver and gold, trout, pike, are very small in this country as they have no muddy shores. Crabs are also small for the same reason, eels, river lampreys and all kinds of sea fish.

The 47th Question.

What kind of dangerous animals are there in the waters?

ALL kinds of snakes, that can swim in the water, these are attacked by the turtles, who eat such as they can overcome. The bite of these snakes is not deadly, but soon passes away after a quick swelling. Upon the land there are rattlesnakes, who in their second year get rattles, and as many years as they get older, so many more rattles, they have fangs, through which they insert poison. They increase by laying eggs, wherewith the sun, however, must do the best part. Their food consist of frogs, toads, weasels. When either man or beast comes too near their young, they crawl into the mother. Next to these are the vipers, grey of color like slate, when they lay in the field they hide their head in the ground, when irritated, they make a noise like an angry cat. Adders are small, quick and redish snakes, their belly is a saffron yellow, and an exceedingly poisonous animal. There are also three kinds of frogs: (1) a middle species, like ours in Germany; (2) a smaller kind, which sings so fine, as the

Art, welche so fein singet, als wie bey uns die Rothstürtzen. Und 3. eine sehr grosse Art, die gibt einen greulichen Gelaut, daß, wo man des Sommers einen daselbst zum Nachbarn hat, so darff man des Nachtwächters und seines Horns nicht, weil er fleissig biß zu Tage aushält mit plerren und ruckesen wie ein junge Ochs.   Andere Kleinigkeiten, die noch im Wasser sind, zu geschweigen.

Die 48. Frage.

Was siehet man dann auff denen Wasser=Flüssen für Thiere schwimmen?

R. SChwanen, Gänse, Kraniche, Endten, Reiger, Adler zweyerley Art: Einen grossen schwartzen mit einen weissen Kopff und rothen Augen, und dann eine kleinere Art, die sich meistens aus dem Wasser nähret. Calecun oder welsche Hüner a. 20. biß 30. Pfund, Phasanen, Patrisen, Tauben, und häuffiges kleines Gevögel, als Spottvogel, Katzvogel, der Vogel rothbords, Carmesin= und Auroraroth.   Und dann ein Wunder aller Rarität, ein Vögelein so groß als ein Glied an einem kleinen Finger, Hummelbart genannt, weilen er keine Flügel von Federn, sondern Hummelsflügel hat.   Sonst sind seine Federn gelb und grün, und hat kurtze Füßgen, schwebt stets in der Lufft, und sauget mit seinem Schnäbelein (welches länger als sein Cör= per ist) das Fette in der Blume und Blüthe, dahero er nicht ehender zu sehen ist, biß Blumen sind, und so bald die Blumen vergehen, so kommet er hinweg, und weiß niemand wo er bleibet, man muß es fast mehr für ein Gespenst und Geist, als vor eine würckliche Creatur, seiner Geschwindigkeit halber, achten.   Sein Nestgen ist so groß wie eine grosse Nußschale.   Sonst gibts Stoßvögel, Habicht, Eulen, Käfer, Raupen, Heuschrecken, Wey= sen und Hornüssen rc.

brown frogs [47] with us, and (3) a very large kind, that emit an abominable bark, so that when one has one of these for a neighbor in the summer, there is no need of any night watch with his horn, as he keeps diligently on until day, with a bellowing and roaring like a young bull. Other trifling things that are in the waters I will omit.

The 48th Question.

What animals are to be seen swimming upon the water courses?

SWANS, geese, cranes, ducks, herons. Of eagles there are two kinds, a great large one with a white head and red eyes, and then a smaller sort which chiefly lives upon the water. *Calecunes* or turkeys of 20 or 30 pounds. Pheasants, partridges, pidgeons and many smaller birds as Mocking bird, catbird, red birds, crimson and aurora red, and then a wonder of all curiosities, a bird no larger than the joint of a little finger, called *Hummelbart* (Humming bird), so called as it has no wings of feathers but *hummel* wings.[48] Otherwise their feathers are yellow and green and they have short legs and constantly hover in the air, and sucks with his bill (which is longer than its body) the richness in the flower and blossom. Therefore they are not to be seen until there are flowers, and as soon as the flowers are over, it goes away, and no one knows where it remains, it seems almost more of a ghost or spirit than an actual creature, on account of its great swiftness. Its nest is as large as a nutshell. In addition there are birds of prey, hawks, owls, bugs, caterpillars, grasshoppers, wasps and hornets.

Die 49. Frage.[20]

Ob nicht [wenn man fromme] Saltzwercker hinein zu
schicken, die die Saltzquelle bey Philadelphia [mit
grossen Vortheil zu gebrauchen und durch
solche denn das gute dort befördert werden könte?] in den Gang brächten?

R. DJESE Saltzquelle [ist meines Erachtens] liegt mehr
dann 10. Meil=Weegs von Philadelphia [nord-west]
Nordwerts, ist [ist aber vor gegenwärtig nichts daran zu
thun] biß dato darumb nicht probirt, dieweilen ein Uberfluß von
Saltz anderwerts eingebracht wird. [es bleibet dieses zum
Profit zu] Die künfftige Ausbreitung und Vermehrung der
Menschen muß auch etwas zu thun haben.

Die 50. Frage.[21]

Ob nicht [so] auch [mit] fromme Bergleute hinein zu
schicken?

R. DJESE könnten noch ehender employrt werden [und
dürfte bald nach ihnen gefragt werden] und könn=
ten immittler Zeit [doch] ihr Leben bey anderer Arbeit und
Viehe Zucht erhalten. [unterhalten]

[20] Question XL in MSS.
[21] Question XLI in MSS.

The 49th Question.

If pious saltworkers[49] were sent over to develop the
saline springs near Philadelphia, could they not be
used with great profit, and through them
further that which is good?

THE saline springs, according to my judgment, are
more than ten miles [50] from Philadelphia toward the
Northwest, but up to the present time they have not been
developed, nor has there even been any attempt to do so, as
there is a superfluity of salt brought here from elsewhere;
so the future development remains for the steadily increasing population here.

The 50th Question.

How about pious miners?

THESE could the more readily find employment here,
and perhaps would soon be in demand. In the
meantime they could support themselves by other labor or
cattle-raising.

Die 51. Frage.[22]

Desideratur eine Geographiſche Beſchreibung von Pensylvanien, [Virginien,] und andern nahe gelege=
nen Ländern und Inſuln ?

R. **DIESES** kan vor gegenwärtig nicht leiſten, ſoll aber, ob
GOtt will, und ich lebe, nechſtens geſchehen. [soll aber
laut meinem Versprechen, ob Gott will und ich lebe, dieselbe erfolgen und zwar *dextre sine præjudicus* und frei-
willigen Fehlern, so entweder aus *ignorantz* und Nach-
lässigkeit oder mangel an *Judicii* entstehen können]

Die 52. Frage.[23]

Wie es mit der Correspondenz in Americam und her=
raus zu halten ?

R. [**DIE** *Correspondentz* muss ihre gewisse Adresse
haben] Dieſe erfordert 4. gewiſſe Adreſſen. Eine
hier in Patria. Die andere in Holland. Die dritte in Engel=
land. Und die vierdte in America. [davon zu einer andern
zeit]

[22] Question XLII in MSS.
[23] Question XLIII in MSS.

The 51st Question.

A geographical description of Pennsylvania and adjacent countries and Islands.

FOR the present this cannot be rendered. But according to my promise, if God will and I live, this shall follow, and indeed *dextre sine praejudicus* and voluntary errors, which could arise either out of ignorance, negligence or lack of *judicum* in which our geographical descriptions thus far abound.

The 52nd Question.

How about correspondence with America and from thence outward.

THE correspondence must have a peculiar address, giving one direction in Germany, another in Holland, a third in England, and a fourth in America. Of this, more at another time.

Die 53. Frage. [24]

Ob nicht allerhand Handwercker darinnen fort kommen?
und welche fürnehmlich?

R. DARAN ist nicht der geringste Zweiffel. Die nothwendigsten aber sind : [welche man im täglichen Gebrauch nicht entrathen kan als] Schmidt, Schlosser, [und die gleichen die in Eisen arbeiten] Schneider, Schuster [Strumpf-Stricker, Rademacher] Zimmerleute [Seiler, welche letzere sonderlich angenehm wegen des grossen Schiffbaues, welcher da angeleget ist] Steinmetzen, [mahler] Maurer, Wagner, Töpffer, Mühlmeister ꝛc. [Kannengieser, Gold-schmiede und dergleichen]

Die 54. Frage. [25]

Wie gute [Erbauliche] Schrifften hinein zu bringen, [in
Englisher und Französischer Sprachen, die *Na-*
***tiones* so in Pennsylvanien, Virginia und New**
Engelland sind, dadurch kräftig zu er-
bauen.] die Landes Inwohner zu er-
bauen?

R. [ERSTLICH ist hier zu merken, wie bekannt, das die beyden Nationen als] Die Englische und Französische Nationen sind schon mit guten Schrifften überhäuffet, [daneben ihre eigenen Scribenten wegen ihres *Styli* und

The 53rd Question.

Whether all kinds of artisans cannot find subsistence
there, and which in particular.

———

ABOUT this there is not the least doubt. The most
necessary ones, however, are those who by daily
usage are indispensable, as smiths, locksmiths, and such
as work in iron. Shoemakers, tailors, stocking-weavers,
wheelwrights, stonecutters, painters, carpenters and rope-
makers would be especially desirable on account of the
extensive ship-building which is carried on here, also
master-millers, pewterers, goldsmiths, potters and the like.

———

The 54th Question.

How to introduce good devout literature in the English
and French languages for an energetic edification
of such nationalities as have settled in Pennsylvania, Virginia and New England.

———

FIRSTLY it is to be remarked, as is well known that
both nations, English and French, are already
overwhelmed with religious literature. Besides, they hold
their own writers in greatest estimation, on account of their
style and national genius. Then, again, no English litera-

genu nationis am meisten æstimiren] Bey uns halten wir der Zeit die H. Schrifft nebst der Kirchen=Histori, und Arndii Büchern Buches genug, für solche, die einer Anleitung vonnöthen haben. Zur Buchdruckrey=Anordnung traue ich allhier nicht bey unserm verführischen, Scoptischen und Satyrischen Zanck=Seculo dardurch nur mehr Unglück und diffidenz angerichtet wird. Doch ist bereits eine zu Philadelphia angerichtet. [So dürfen auch keine Englische Schriften ausserhalb Engelland gedruckt in Engelland eingeführt werden. Zudem *observire* ich bey Gelegenheit der Päbstlichen religion etwas, welches mir in gewissen Stücken nicht ungereimt vorkommt, nemlich, dass sie aus einem *stratagemate ecclesiastico politico* denen Leuten viel äusserliche Gottesdienste, Feyer-Tage, Messen und dergleichen aufgeleget haben; und ob'sie wohl über die Schrift die *Patres* und *statuta ecclesiae* zu ihrem *canone* nehmen, so lässet doch der ohne das mit Gottesdienst überhaufte Hauffe der (der) Layen das *scrutinium fidei* der *auctoritati virorum* gern über und bleiben also niedrig und gebeugt. Dahero ihr äusserliches Regiment nicht mit so viel Secten und Rotten verunruhiget worden kan. *America* hält den Menschen unter äusserlicher Übung : Adam bauet das Land und wartet seines Viehes, welches lauter Buchstaben und Bücher sind, dabei ihn sein Schöpfer selbst in der Danksagung *ex tempore* lehret und aufsagen heisset. Ist Zeit übrig, so is die heilige Schrift nebst der Kirchen-Historie und Arndii Büchern Buchs genug, vor solche die einer Anleitung von nöthen haben. Zur Druckerey wollte ich wol rathen weil ich aber sehe den greulichen Missbrauch und daher entstehendes Ubel welcher doch umb dessentwillen man *rebus sic stantibus* in Europa nicht entbehren kan : so traue ich unserm verführerischen sceptischen und satyrischen Zank-*Seculo* nicht viel, wollte auch nicht gern helfen Unglück anrichten nachdem ich schon proben davon

ture printed outside of England is permitted to be imported into the country. I will observe upon this occasion something concerning the Papal religion which in certain particulars does not seem to me inconsistent, namely, that they have imposed upon their people, out of a *Stratagemate ecclesiastico politico*, many outward forms of worship, holy days, masses and the like; and although they take for their canons those of the priests and *statuta ecclesiæ* above those of Holy writ, yet the mass of the laity are not burdened with divine services but gladly leave the *Scrutinium fidei* to the *auctoritati virorum*, and remain lowly and humble. Therefore their outward organization cannot be disturbed by so many sects and factions. America holds man under an external training.

Adam tills his land and tends his cattle, all of which are letters and books, wherein his creator personally instructs him in thanksgiving, and asks him to remember what he has learned. If there is time to spare, then the Holy writ, together with sacred history and Arndt's [51] works, are books enough for such as have heed of guidance when in dire straits.

As to a printing office, I would well approve of one; but when I see the abominable abuse made of it and the resulting evils (which we, however, for that reason, *rebus sic stantibus*, cannot spare in Europe), I do not trust our seductive, sceptical and satirical quarrelsome *seculum*. Further, I should not like to be a party to cause any calamity, as I have already seen proof thereof in America. But I should not object provided strict and accurate regulations of the press were enforced. According to my latest advices from Pennsylvania, from a letter dated September 17, 1699, I learn that besides the printing office in New York, another has been set up in Philadelphia. [52] At the

auch in America gesehen: es wäre dann dass man scharfe
und genaue Ordnung des Drucks halber machen wollte.
Laut letzterer Brieffe vom 7 September 1699 aus Pennsylvanien verstehe, dass man über die Druckerey in Newjork
noch eine in Philadelphia angeleget hat, bey welcher Gelegenheit nächst künftig einige teutsche Schriften in englisch und frantzösisch daselbst übersetzen und also zum
Druck noch gut befinden und Vermögen wird befördern
können, bis der Drucker sich auch mit teutschen Buchstaben wird versehen haben.]

Die 55. Frage. [26]

**Wie man Leute eines rechten Philadelphischen Geistes
von [Schweden, Engelländern, Deutschen, und
von] allen Religionen, so darinnen sind, uffzu-
suchen habe, die zu Beförderung des Wercks
des HErren einander die Hand biethen können?**

R. **D**AS ist eine schwere Frage. Das weiß ich: Wann alle
Secten und Partheyen ihre Mutter-Maale wolten verlaugnen, und mit einander ins gleiche Recht durch eine Brüder-
liche Resignirte Liebes-Resolution eingehen, so dörffte man sich
nicht viel bedencken: Gottes Werck würde sich selbsten treiben;
Und zum wenigsten könnte es von uns, als von uns nicht aufge-
halten werden. Inzwischen bekommt ein guter Meister viel Kun-
den, darum muß ein Anfang seyn, und die Liebe muß eine Arbeit
haben, dann findet sich das Mittel durch Mittel.

[26] Question XLVI in MSS.

earliest opportunity I shall translate several German writ-
ings into English and French, and print them there according to circumstances and ability, until the printer is also
supplied with German type.[83]

The 55th Question.

How to seek out persons imbued with a true Philadelphian spirit from among the Swedes, English,
Germans, and religious persuasions who are
there, and would be willing to extend
their hands to one another in the
furtherance of the word
of the Lord.

THIS is a difficult question. I do know, however,
that if all sects and parties would abjure their
birth marks and enter with one accord into a resolution of
resigned brotherly love, one would not then need to have
any doubt that God's work would accomplish itself, or at
least it could not be checked by or of us. In the meantime a good master gains many customers. Therefore
there must be a beginning, and charity must be given a
certain task, then will be found means by means. I know
of several good friends there, whose good intentions are
greater than their outward actions would warrant. God,

Ich weiß einige gute Freunde allda, die mehr im guten Willen, als in der äusserlichen That vermögen. GOtt, der aller Menschen Hertzen in seiner Hand hat, und dieselbe wie Wasser [bäche] leitet, weiß einfältiges lauteres Vornehmen zu secundiren.

Die 56. Frage.[27]

Wie alt die Wilden werden?

R. **VOr** diesem 100. Jahr, heut zu Tage 60. oder 70. Jahr, wegen verlassener Diät. [Es sind wenige nun mehro von denen, die wir kennen, die 60–70 jahre alt sind. Vor diesem sind sie 100 jahre alt geworden. Die ursache davon erhellet aus schon angeführten.]

Die 57. Frage.[28]

Ob ihrer Weiber einander in der Geburt beystehen?

R. **NEin** [So viel ich Verstanden geschieht es nicht] sondern sie verbergen sich gantz allein in einem vorher ausgesehenen Orte, und doch gleichwohl sihet man nicht ein einiges ungestaltes Kind oder Krippel. [Ob nun dieses die jungen weibern auch also und zu aller Zeit thun, habe aus der Acht gelassen. Davon mehrere Gewissheit so wir leben]

[27] Question XLVII in MSS.
[28] Question XLVIII in MSS.

who has all human hearts in his hands and directs them like a water course, is ready to further any pure and simple undertaking.

The 56th Question.

To what age do the savages attain?

THERE are but few of them known to us who are sixty to seventy years old. Formerly they lived to the age of a hundred. The causes for this appear from what has already been said.

The 57th Question.

Do the women assist each other during parturition?

SO far as I have understood, this is not done; but they betake themselves entirely alone to some previously selected spot. However, at the same time, you cannot find a single deformed child or cripple amongst them. Whether the young women follow the same course at all times, I have been unmindful of. Concerning this, more information, if we live.

Die 58. Frage.[29]

Wie sie es mit denen gantz kleinen Kindern halten?

R. **Sie** [die kleinen Kinder] werden uff eine kurtze Zeit an ein Bretgen gebunden, darauf sie ein kleines Fellelein binden, und es mit eben dergleichen zudecken, damit sies desto besser auf dem Rucken tragen, und desto gewisser halten können wann sie [indem sie dieselben fast allezeit] saugen. [lassen weil sie über die Massen viel Milch haben und doch nur kaltes wasser trincken. Das Haupt und den Körper des Knaben salben sie mit guten fett von Thieren.]

Die 59. Frage.[30]

Was für Flüsse der Orten sind?

R. [**Die** Nahmen der Flüsse sind meist Indianisch, deswegen verspare ich sie mit ihrer *Etymologie* und anzahl bis auf weitern Bescheid] America ist wie ein durchwässerter Garten von grossen und kleinen Flüssen, und schönen Brunnquellen. Die Etimologiam urd Anzahl solcher Flüsse verspahre ich vor diesesmal, biß zu meiner wieder Hineinkunfft, und schrifftlichen Bericht.

29 Question XLIX in MSS.
30 Question L in MSS.

The 58th Question.

How do they care for their infants?

THE infants are bound for a short time, on boards or bark covered with soft fur, with which they also cover them, so that they can the better carry them on their backs. They let them nurse almost continuously as they have nourishment beyond all measure, and yet they drink nothing but cold water. They anoint the heads and bodies of the boys with some good animal fat.

The 59th Question.

What rivers are there ?

THE names of most of the rivers are of Indian origin. Therefore I will reserve the etymology and number for some future occasion. Otherwise America is like an irrigated garden, full of large and small rivers and great and small springs.

Die 60. Frage.[31]

Wie sie gebrauchet werden?

Responsio fimilitet differtur. [Die Antwort wird bis
aufs künftige versparet]

Die 61. Frage.[32]

Wie sie ihre Fischerey halten?

R. [**D**IESE bestehet hauptsachlich in folgenden Arten,
erstlich] 1. **Mit dem Angel.** 2. **Machen sie Dammen
von Steinen** [in die Flüsse, wie sie beginnen seichte zu werden in dieser Form: ‿⁄‿⁄‿ Durch die Canäle fället
das aufgehaltene wasser ab und der Strom bekomt eine
force, am ende des Canals stehet ein grosser Korb von Reif-
staben gemacht. Da treibet der Strom den Fisch, so herun-
ter gehet, hinein, welcher Korb so gesetzet ist, dass der
Fisch nicht kan wieder zurück gehen.] **und includiren die
Fische.** 3. **Binden sie eine lange Reyhe Reiser mit dem Laub zusammen** [wie ein Netz] **und ziehens durchs Wasser, damit sie die
Fische in eine Enge zusamm jagen, und mit den Händen erdappen.**
[Auch haben sie ihre Kähne, welche von Rinden von
Bäumen gemacht und mit Wildem Hanf verbunden und
mit Moos verstopfet sind, in dieselben treten sie und halten
bey stillem Wetter an einem solchen Ort, da sie wissen,
wo sich der Fish, *Stör* genannt, aufhalt; da haben sie ein
scharfes Eisen (vorher einen scharfen harten Stein) an
einer langen Stange an einem Strick festgemacht; sobald

---

[31] Question LI in MSS.
[32] Question LII in MSS.

The 60th Question.

How are they utilized?

THIS answer is reserved for the future.

The 61st Question.

How is Fishing Followed?

THIS consists chiefly of the following methods :
Firstly, angling ; secondly making dams of stones
in the rivers where they begin to get shallow, in this manner ‾\/‾\/‾. Through these conduits the checked
water flows and the current gathers in force. At the end
of each conduit a large wicker basket is placed, the current
drives the descending fish through the conduit into the
basket, which is set at such an angle that the fish cannot
return. Thirdly, they tie a long row of green branches
with their leaves together like a net, and drag those
through the water so as to drive the fish into a convenient
corner, where they can catch them with their hands.
Fourthly, they also have their canoes, made out of the
bark of trees, bound together with wild hemp and caulked
with mosses, in which they stand up in still weather at such
places which they know that the Stör [53] fish frequents ; then
they have a sharp iron (formerly a sharp-pointed stone) on
a long pole, to which is fastened a rope. Now, as soon as

sie nun einen dergleichen Fisch, welcher sich zuweilen sonnet und ruhet, gewahr worden, können sie durch ihre Geschwindigkeit ihm bald eins versetzen, das er herauf komt und den Bauch in die Höhe kehret. Dergleichen Fische fangen sie zuweilen in einem Tage so viel, dass sie eine gantze Nachbarschaft damit versehen können.] Sie haben auch Kähne von ausgeholten Bäumen, und die Ritzen mit Mos verstopffet, in welche sie tretten, und die Stör fangen.

Die 62. Frage. [33]

Wie die Wilden ihre Jagten anstellen?

R. DEREN wilden Thiere bemächtigen sie sich geschwinde durch ihr schnelles und anhaltendes Lauffen, und durch ihr Geschoß. Einige Thiere suchen sie des Nachts bey hellem Mondscheine. [auf die Bäume zu jagen,] Die wilde Katzen schiesens mit Pfitschepfeilen. Die Amyhibia als Ratzen, Marter und dergleichen, fangen sie zu Nachts in Fallen, fast wie unsere Marter=Fallen.

Die 63. Frage. [34]

Was vor zahme [und wilde] Thier es bey ihnen gebe?

R. FAST alle, die wir hieraussen haben, ausgenommen, keinen Esel haben sie drinnen, welcher ihnen doch sehr nutzlich wäre, indeme man die Pferde mit dem schweren Läste tragen verderbet, welchen die Natur mehr Stärcke in denen Schultern [und Füsse] als in dem Rucken gegeben, da hingegen der Esel im

[33] Question LIII in MSS.
[34] Question LIV in MSS.

they see such a fish, which occasionally suns itself and rests, they are enabled by their extreme dexterity to spear it, so that it turns its belly upward and comes to the surface. Of these fish they often catch so many in a day, that the whole neighborhood is supplied therewith.

The 62nd Question.

Concerning their hunting.

THEY overpower the wild beasts quickly by their rapid and continuous running, together with their missiles. Some animals they capture on the trees in the bright moonlight. Several of the amphibious beasts they catch at night in traps, similar to our traps for martens.[54]

The 63rd Question.

What kind of animals are there, both domestic and wild?

WITH some exceptions, just the same as with us here.[55] Among these exceptions is the jackass, which would be very useful there. The horses, whom nature has given more strength in their shoulders and legs than in their backs, are ruined by the heavy burdens they carry.[56] On the contrary the jackass is strong in his back and con-

Rücken starck ist, und mit schlechtem Futter sich befriedigen lässt. [Die Nahmen der Thiere so da und nicht hie sind, samt der *Etymologie* davon soll künftig mit folgen.]

Die 64. Frage. [35]

Was für unterschiedliche Vögel darinnen?

R.   JSt theils oben beantwortet, und sind deren viel Arten dort, die nicht hier, und viele hier, welche dorten nicht sind. Davon ins künfftig.

Die 65. Frage. [36]

Wie man sich gegen die Bären, und andere wilde Thiere verwahre?

R.   DJE wilden Thiere hat GOtt mit Forcht geschrecket, daß sich kein Mensch ihrenthalben zu besorgen hat, [Dahero auch unsere zahme Thiere die wilden wenig *æstimiren* und wessen ihre Jungen vor der andern Gewalt wohl zu bewahren. Ausser der Schafe, vor welchen die Wölfe ohne hülffe der Menschen und hunde nicht erschrecken und sich vergeblich abweisen lassen.] vor Schlangen [man vielerley Art] hat man sich im Sommer in acht zu nehmen, die doch [wiewohl sie insgemein] ein Geräusche machen, und flüchtig werden ehe man zu ihnen kommt, dahero sie nicht leichtlich den Menschen schaden. [Es sey denn den Vorwitzigen und unachtsamen; doch sind die *Exempel* rar]

[35] Question LV in MSS.
[36] Question LVI in MSS.

tent with indifferent feed. The names of the animals which are there [57] and not here [58] together with the etymology of the same will follow in the future.

The 64th Question.

What kinds of birds are there?

OF these there are many species that are not here[59] and many here that are not there. Whereof also in the future.

The 65th Question.

How to protect oneself against bears and other wild beasts?

THE Lord has so terrified the wild beasts with fear that no man need be apprehensive upon their account. For this reason our domestic animals show but little fear for the wild ones, and know well how to protect their young against their violence. The sheep are an exception, as the wolves cannot be frightened off or repulsed without the aid of men and dogs. Snakes, of which there are many kinds, one has to be very careful of in summer, although they usually make some noise or take flight before one comes up to them. Therefore they do not often harm any-one, unless he be indiscreetly curious or heedless. But such examples are rare.

Die 66. Frage.[37]

Wormit die Wilden bißhero von denen Europäern ge=
ärgert? und noch schlimmer gemacht worden? [und
wie solche Aergerniss zu emendiren]

R. Sie haben bey der Gegenwart und Lebens=Art der Euro=
päer gelernet unordentlich mit zu leben, im Essen,
Trincken, Sauffen, Fluchen, Lügen, Betrügen, einer hat dem
andern die Gelegenheit gezeiget, die Europär haben ihnen Bran=
dewein, Bier, und andere Materialia hinein gebracht, so nun die
Wilden mit Begierde suchen, und obs ihnen schon durch Gesetze
verbotten ist, so wissen sies doch mit Lust zu sich zu bekommen,
repete hic quæst. 39. R. [Vors erste kan das kein Aergerniss heissen, das sie bey der Gegenwart und Lebens-Art
der Europeer Gelegenheit nehmen unordentlich zu werden,
sonst könte sich auch ein Kind des Aergernisses nicht
erwehren. Denn wenn dasselbe sein Muss isset zu seiner
Nahrung, so mag es geschehen, dass dieses die Katze
gewahr wird, durch dessen Geruch und Geschmack sie
alle gelegenheit suchet ohne Hinderniss zum Verdruss
ihres eigenen Magens und derer, die im Zimmer sind, an-
füllet. Die Europeer haben zwar Bier und Brantewein
hineingebracht, wer kan es aber helfen, dass die wilden
davon zu viel nehmen. Man hat allerhand Gesetz und
Ordnung gemacht, wie viel man denselben reichen solle.
Doch wissen sie es mit List zu bekommen, wiewol auch
einige gewinnsüchtige Leute sind, die ihnen in das Holtz
profits halber dergleichen Getränke zukommen lassen.
Und weil sie es nicht allezeit haben, noch haben konnen,
weil ihr Verdienst nicht gross ist, so ist die Natur desto

---

[37] Question LVII and LVIII in MSS.

The 66th Question.

Wherein the savages have thus far been made specially worse in whole or in part by the Europeans,
and how such scandal may be amended.

———

FIRSTLY, it cannot be called a scandal that they take
the opportunity of becoming disorderly from the
presence and manner of living of the Europeans, else a
child could not refrain from scandal. For when it eats its
pap for its sustenance, it may happen that a cat becomes
aware of it, and by its sense of taste and smell seeks every
opportunity when without hindrance it can gorge itself, to
the vexation of its own stomach and those who are in the
room. The Europeans certainly did bring in beer and
brandy, but who can help it that the savages take too much
thereof ? All kinds of laws and regulations have been
made as to the quantity that might be given to them.
However, they know how to obtain it by their cunning,
although there are some mercenary people who for gain
furnish them with drink in the forest. As they do not have
it at all times nor can always obtain it (for their earnings
are not large) their nature upon this account makes them
still more ravenous, and when opportunity offers they cannot keep themselves within bounds.

It is said that in Carolina, before the advent of the
French, strict regulations were enforced, whereby it was
absolulely forbidden under a heavy penalty to give the
savages any beer, wine or brandy. According to my
judgment, the most harm is done by a pack of unscrupu-
lous, dissolute and corrupt peddlers [59] of the English,

begieriger darauf und können sich in der gelegenheit
nicht mässigen. Man sagt, dass in Carolina ehe und
bevor die Frantzosen dahin gekomen, genaue Ordnung sei
gehalten worden, darinnen absolut und bey hoher Strafe
verbothen gewesen, denen Wilden Bier, Wein und Brantewein zu geben. Der meiste Schaden ist meines Erachtens
geschehen durch einige gewissenlose, liederliche und faule
Schacherer von Engelländern, Schweden, in specie Frantzosen, welche die Wilden übervortheilt, und sie durch
practiquen theils schüchtern theils listig gemacht, das sie
biss weilen sich zu keiner *conversation* einlassen wollen,
biss weilen lieber solche liederlich *compagnie* erleiden,
welche sie entweder mit starkem Getränke unterhalten und
es ihnen weit nachbringen, oder ihnen von unseren Königen
närrische *Historischen* einbilden und allerlei neue Zeitung
erzählen welches Aergerniss aber durch einen besseren
Umgang leicht wird zu heben seyn. Was sie sonst von
den Europeern angenommen siehe oben *quaest.* XXXIX.]

Die 67. Frage.[38]

Wie man lauter nutzliche Künste und Wissenschaften in Americam bringen könne? [Die Bösen unnützen und unnöthigen weg lassen]

R. Hierbey muß man Unanimiter erst erkennen, was man
bißhero in der Ubung in der Gottseeligkeit nach allen
Ständen nutzlich oder schädlich gefunden, und dann weil das Land
dort noch einfältig, die im Römischen Reich præter necessitatem
multiplicirte Entia lieber hinweg lassen, damit man die anti-

---

[38] Question LIX in MSS.

Swedish and especially of French nationality, who defraud
the savages, and intimidate them by their practices, or else
make them so cunning that they often refuse to enter into
conversation, and prefer such dissolute company as either
entertains them with strong drink, or sends it to them, or
conceive foolish stories about our kings and tell them all
kinds of new tidings; a scandal which can easily be dis-
pelled by better associations. What they have otherwise
acquired from the Europeans, see question XXXIX supra.

The 67th Question.

How to introduce purely advantageous arts and
sciences into America, and eliminate the
evil and useless ones.

HEREWITH one must first *unanimiter* understand
what has been found to be useful or harmful thus
far in the practice of godliness toward all estates, and
then, as the country is still in a state of simplicity, those in
the Holy Roman Empire [62] also *præter necessitatem multi-
plicierte Entia*, had better omit that one the *antiquam
simplicitatem* in *antiqua Sanctirate* can the better take into
account. A certain project (as a guide for constructing
others) will be added at the ending.

quam simplicitatem in antiqua Sanctirate deſto beſſer in acht nehmen könne, ein gewiſſes Project, umb darnach andere ſelbſt zu machen, ſoll am Ende beygefüget werden.

Die 68. Frage. [39]

Wie das Land zu ſeinen rechten Gebrauch und Nutzen zu bringen?

R. DER in das Land kommende Menſch ſoll ſich mit Leib und Seel GOtt aufopffern, allein deſſen Glory und Ehre ſuchen, und alſo in Seegen und Frieden dieſe Erde beſitzen, damit America auch einen Saamen habe, der dem HErrn diene, und in Gerechtigkeit ſeinen Weinberg baue und pflantze, dann wohl iſt dem Volck des der HErr ein GOtt iſt. [Der einige rechte Nutzen und Gebrauch eines Landes, in Ansehen eines Menschen, ist, dass derselbe darinne dem Leibe nach als in einem Gefängniss nothdürftig unterhalten werde, bis zu seiner Wiederbringung in seinen vorigen Stand. Mittler Zeit soll er der Creatur als ein Herr vorstehen, dieselbe zur Ehre Gottes auf opfern, und also im Seegen und Frieden die Erde besitzen. Solches solte ja auch billig bey *singulis individuis* in *America* beobachtet werden, aber weil das reich Gottes selbst gleich ist einem Netze, das voll guter und böser Fische was wil das *corruptibile terrae corpus* nicht seyn? Doch wie die adern der besten *Metalle* durch die grosse und finstere Massen der Erden durch laufen und dieselbe gleichsam durch ihre Dämpfe vermittelst der Sonnen und des Mondes *tingiren* und saltzen. Also lauft die Lebens linie und das Geschlechts-Register

-----

[39] Question LX in MSS.

The 68th Question.

How to develop the country and bring about its proper uses and advantages.

THE only proper use and advantage of a country in the sight of man, according to the body, is that therein, as one in a prison, they be supported with what is absolutely necessary, until a restoration to their former condition. In the meantime one should present the creature as a man, and offer it up for the glory of God, and at the same time enjoy the earth in peace and tranquility. Such could be truly observed about single individuals in America.[61] But as the realm of God is like a net that is full of fish both good and bad, what can we expect from the earth's corruptible body? But, as the veins of the most precious metals run through the great and dark masses of the earth, and by means of the sun and moon as it were, bedew and season the same by their exhalations, so also runs the vital line and the genealogical pedigree of our Lord Jesus Christ, in single cases, as firstlings of the spirit, through all nations and races, according as the nations become pregnant in the faith of Abraham. Consequently America will also produce seed, that will serve the Lord, hold forth in righteousness, and plant the land and vineyards. In the meantime let Tyre and Sidon plant cities for their children, and Merchants of Merari, or such as deem themselves wise, seek ever according to their impulse and manner, their wisdom's part. We say, happy are they who go thus. But fortunate are the people whose Lord is God. What otherwise concerns the order

unseres Herrn Jesu Christi in einzelnen Nahmen, als Erst-
linge des Geistes durch alle Völker und Geschlechter darnach die Volker als in dem Glauben Abrahams gesegnet
werden. Also wird *America* auch Saamen haben, der
dem Herrn dienet und in Gerechtigkeit predigen, Land
und Weinberge pflantzen wird. Es baue und pflantze inzwischen *Tyron* und *Sidon* ihren Kindern Städte, und die
Kaufleute von *Merari* oder die sich klug dünken, suchen
immerhin nach ihren Trieb und Weise ihrer Weissheit
Theil. Wir sagen wohl dem, dem es also gehet, aber
wohl dem volk des der Herr ein Gott ist.] Die Ordnung
der eusserlichen Cultivirung dieses Landes, lässet sich nicht also in
die Kürtze fassen, noch auch ohne die würckliche Application recht
verstehen, weilen das Vorhersehen einige Dinge grösser, und
einige kleiner machet, als sie in der That selbst sind.

Die 69. Frage.[40]
**Wann Christliche Leute hinein [kommen] wollen, die
grobe eusserliche Arbeit nicht verrichten können, wie
man sie zu gebrauchen wisse, und wie sie sich
nähren können. Ob durch Information,
oder noch uff andere Weise?**

R. Fromme Leute, die keiner harten Arbeit können vorstehen,
und auch keine Mittel haben, die müssen es auf den
Glauben der Sperlinge, und des Lilien auf dem Felde anfangen,
dann kan GOtt unsere Seele starck machen, so kan er auch unsern
Leib starck machen, weil er ihn auch von den Todten auferwecken
will, wer thut was er kan, und lebt in Gottesfurcht, den will der

[40] Question LXI in MSS.

of outward civilization of the land is not to be compre-
hended by any abbreviated form, nor rightly understood
without an actual application, as the preponderance of certain things makes them appear greater or smaller that they
actually are.

The 69th Question.

If Christian people want to come in, who could not
perform the ordinary rough work, how could they
be made useful, and sustain themselves? —
If through information or otherwise.

DEVOUT persons, who cannot undertake hard labor
nor have any means, they must begin with the
faith of the sparrow, and the lilies of the field, for as the
Lord can strengthen our soul, so can he also quicken our
body, even as he will awaken it from the dead. Whosoever doeth what he can, and liveth in the fear of the Lord,
him will the good Lord maintain. He that hath learned
something in his youth can inform others who are ignorant.
Enfeebled persons could also be placed so as to keep an
oversight over the household and the government of children, whereby they could obtain the necessaries of life.
Christian people who have no means, nor the capacity
for outside work, must begin upon the faith of the wild
animals, the sparrows and the lilies of the field; not that
they should withdraw entirely from the divine order
and their obligations thereto. On the other hand, to

liebe **GOtt** schon ernähren. Wer etwas in seiner Jugend gelernet hat, der kan andere Unwissende schon informiren. Auch könnte man schwachgliedrige Leute zur Aufsicht über Haußhaltungen und Kinderzucht setzen, darbey sie ihre Nothdurfft finden können.

[Christliche Leute die gar keine Mittel, auch kein Vermögen zu äusserlicher Arbeit haben, müssen es auf den Glauben der wilden Thiere, der Sperlinge und der Lilien auf dem Felde anfangen nicht dass sie sich der Ordnung Gottes und ihrer Schuldigkeit gantz entziehen wolten, hingegen anderen alleine eine Last aufgeleget wissen, das wäre zum wenigsten gegen die aufrichtige liebe. Denn kan Gott unsere Seele stark machen, so kan er auch unseren Leib Stärcken weil er ihn auch von den Todten auferwecken wil. David war nur ein schwacher Hirten-Knabe und doch hat der Herr seine Hände lehren streiten und seine Finger einen eisernen Bogen spannen. Wer thut, was er kan, den muss der liebe Gott wohl ernehren, weil Er's gesagt hat und auch thun kan. Zur information könte wohl Rath werden vor etliche; so könte man auch schwachen Leuthen die Aufsicht über Hausshaltung und Kinder anvertrauen, dabei sie ihre Nothdurft finden können doch wird es auch den Schwachen, höchst zu *recomendiren* seyn, dass sie sich wie die Kinder *gradatim* zu einer mehreren motion und Arbeit gewöhnen, weil die Gesundheit vieler von Mutter-Leibe an kränklichen Körper auf solche Weise kan *recuperiret* und erhalten werden, davon ich mich selbst zu einem lebendigen Beweisthum darstellen kan.]

thrust themselves as a burden upon others, that would at least be far from sincere charity. For, as God can strengthen the soul, so can He also strengthen our bodies, as well as resurrect them from the dead. David was only a weak shepherd boy, and yet the Lord endowed his hands with strength and his fingers with power to draw an iron bow. He that doeth what he can, him the dear Lord will amply support, as he hath said it, and can also do it. For the information of some, counsel might be of avail. Thus, delicate persons might be entrusted with an oversight of a household or of children, whereby they could gain the necessaries of life; although it might be well to recommed to the weak and delicate that they, like children, should gradually take more and more exercise, so as to accustom themselves to labor, as the health of many who were sickly from their birth was recuperated and maintained by these means. Of which I can present myself as a living example.

Die 70. Frage.[41]

Wann neue Colonien hinein kommen, ob ſie ſich zu den alten ſchlagen müſſen, oder ob ſie ſelbſt eine neue Stadt anrichten können?

R. **Es** iſt rathſam, daß ſich die neu=Ankommende durch die Erfahrung anderer weiſen, und ihre eigene Weißheit fahren laſſen, Experto credo Ruperto. Des Raums halber können ſie gar wohl in den alten Colonien bleiben, und von denen, die ſchon etwas gewiſſes in ihren Seelen gefaſſet haben, mehr lernen und abſehen, als in Camagna aus der leeren Lufft. [Es ist rathsam, dass sich neue Ankommer durch die Erfahrung anderer weisen, und ihre eigene Weissheit, welche ihrem besten bisweilen *praejudicirlich*, fahren lasse, *expert credo Ruperto*. Des Raumes halber können, sie noch wohl in den alten *Colonien* bleiben, der Freiheit halber können sie auch neue Städte anlegen, doch ist es gut, dass man die alten unvermögenden, welche ihre Dienste schon in dieser welt gethan und etwas gewisses in ihren Seelen haben auf denjenigen was vorher bearbeitet ist, zurücke lässt und nur die Jungen unter weiser Aufsicht und Anführung weiter fortsendet doch so dass man ihnen in einer kleinen Tagereise *assistiren* könne, so bliebe die jugend auch fein in einerley Weise und lernete sich nicht aufs neue umsehen nach den Töchtern der Menschen mann dürfte auch auf solche weise im 3ten und 4ten Glied eine bessere generation sehen, und dem Herren darinnen von Geschlecht zu Geschlecht Lob bekommen.]

---

[41] Question LXII in MSS.

The 70th Question.

When new Colonies come over, must they join one
of the old ones, or must they build a
new town for themselves.

IT is advisable that newcomers profit by the experience
of others, and abandon their own wisdom, which is frequently prejudiced *experto crede Ruperto.* So far as the
room is concerned, they might still remain with the old
colonies. For the sake of freedom they might found new
towns. Yet it is advisable that the aged and indigent, who
have long since fulfilled their mission in this world, and
have an assurance within their souls, be left where the
ground is already cultivated, and merely push forward the
youth under the supervision of a tutor, yet not further than
where assistance could reach them within a short day's
journey. Then the youth would also remain genteely in
the ways of simplicity, and learn not to seek anew after
the daughters of man. We might in this manner obtain
better species in the third and fourth generations, and the
Lord obtain praise from generation to generation.

Die 71. Frage.[42]

Was für Vorschläg zu einer solchen neuen Colonia zu thun seye?

R. DESES kan ohne Consens und Beyrathen derer Herrn Goubernatoren im Lande nicht geschehen, diesen ist der Mangel der alten Welt bekannt, und diese haben mit einem nüchternen Gemüthe schon abgesehen, wie sie die neue Welt an Gottesfurcht und guten Gebäuden gerne angeordnet hätten. Den Vorschuß an eusserlichen Mitteln wird niemand thun, sondern das Land muß ihm selbst thun, und Gottes Schickung. Das Werck des HErrn aber wird Supernaturaliter fortgepflantzet und erhalten, es muß sich nur leiden, schmiegen und stille halten, stets im Kampffe bestehen. Mit unserer eusserlichen Menschen Hülffe ist wenig auszurichten, wo aber Gottes Geist in die Hertzen einleuchtet, da gehet alles herrlich von statten. [Die *resolution* vieler Gemüther mit eins, welche die Mangel der alten Welt in nüchtern Gemüth einsehen, könten allerhand Vorschläge machen, aus welchen die besten zu erwählen wären, der Vorschuss äusserlichen Mittel wie viel und woher derselbe zu nehmen, sorgete ich gar nicht, weil das Land selbst viel Vorschuss thut und Gottes Werck muss sich ohne das mehr durch die Welt schmiegen in Leid und Kampf, als dass es von denselben mit ernstlicher Hülfe solte befordert werden.]

[42] Question LXIII in MSS.

The 71st Question.

What suggestions are to be made to such a new colony?

THIS cannot be done in this country without the consent and advice of the Lord Governors, to whom the deficiencies of the old world are known, and these have to consider in sober earnest, how the new world is to be advanced in the fear of the Lord, and by suitable structure. No advance of material means will be offered by anyone, but the country must furnish this itself with the dispensation of providence. The work of the Lord, however, will be extended and maintained supernaturally, we must only continue in the warfare with endurance, humility and patience. With outward human help little is to be accomplished, but where the Lord's spirit illuminates the heart there all succeeds gloriously.

[The resolutions of many dispositions with one that in sober mind understanding the shortcomings of the old world, could make all manner of propositions, from which the best could be selected. The advancement of material means, how much and whence they are to be obtained, I give no consideration. The country itself offers much for one's advancement, and the work of the Lord must be extended, without any further cringing through life in sorrow and strife, but with the earnest assistance of the same.]

Die 72. Frage. [43]

**Wie in specie es damit einzurichten daß die Nachkom=
men sich einer guten Ordnung in allen Stücken
mögten zu erfreuen haben?**

R. **Auf einen guten Grund bauet sich ein gutes Hauß, und
wann dem Verderben gesteuert ist, so wächset die Gerech=
tigkeit überschwenglich.** [doch muss man in unserer Zeit der
graduum templi Salomonia nicht vergessen, dass man von
einem nicht mehr fördere als er leisten konne, noch auch
durch gesetzlichen Vorzug und Ordnung einer solchen
Wahl sich merken lasse, dadurch an einer Seite *Ambition*
und Herrschaft an der anderen Seite heimlicher Neid und
Verleumdung oder Gegensatz entstehe, viel mehr still-
schweigend durch Weissheit denen Starken und Schwachen
zur Besserung gefalle und weil sich diese Welt durch
autoritate publica nicht regieren lässt, so könte man dieselbe der Kirchen halber einem treuen Menschen samt 4
Altesten anbefehlen, äusserlichen Dinge halber aber 1 oder
2 nach den Englischen Rechten gesetzte Friedens-Richter
zu sorgfältiger Aufsicht und treuen Ordnern, so würde
nicht leicht ein *Casus* fürfallen damit man die hohe Landes
Obrigkeit weiter beschweren müsste.] **Es muß Auctoritas
aliqua publica dabey seyn, die Kirchen=Sachen muß man einem
geistlichen Vorsteher nebst 4. Aeltisten befehlen, die da nicht auf
einer Seiten ambition und Herrschafft suchen, und auff der
andern Seiten heimlichen Neid und Verleumbdung, der Sanfft=
müthige JEsus muß ihnen aus dem Hertzen und aus dem Ange=
sichte leuchten. In eufserlichen weltlichen Dingen nach den Eng=
lischen Rechten und Gesetzen Friedens=Richter zu sorgfältiger
Aufsicht verordnen.**

[43] Question LXIV in MSS.

The 72nd Question.

How in particular to make arrangements so that those who follow may enjoy good order in every way.

αPON solid ground a good house may be built, and when depravity is checked, then righteousness increases boundlessly, although in our time we must not forget the *graduum templi Salomonis*, and not demand more of any person than he is capable of. In making such selection by lawful preference and regulation, we must remember that thereby upon one side we have ambition and domination, and upon the other side either secret envy or calumny which appears in contradistinction to the other.

Better silence in wisdom, guide the strong and feeble toward reformation, and as the world will not be ruled by public authority, the same on account of the church might be entrusted into the hands of some trusty and faithful man, together with four elders. But for outward affairs let one or two Justices of the Peace be installed according to the English law, as careful supervisors and trusty regulators. Then a case would rarely occur which would have to be appealed to the supreme authority.[64]

There must be at least some public authority. Church affairs must be ordered by a spiritual leader with four elders, who neither seek ambition and power upon one side, nor practice secret envy and calumniation upon the other. The meek and gentle Jesus must be in their hearts, and shine out of their countenance. In outward worldly matters, a Justice of the Peace must keep a careful oversight according to the English rights and laws.

Die 73. Frage.[44]

In was für Ordnung die jetzigen Colonien stehen? wie
sie vom Magistrat regieret werden? wie dem Bösen
gewehret, und das Gute belohnet wird?

R. Die jetzigen Colonien werden unter Gubernatoribus, nach
den Englischen Gesetzen, regirt, [und gefallen mir
dieselbigen sehr wohl, weil sie die Freiheit geben und
nicht absolut tyrannisch sind, so weiss ich auch dass nach
der *instruction* der Friedens-Richter in einer derselben
mehr *Autoritat* in *Publico* das Böse zu strafen hat, als kein
Prediger hierin öffentlich nehmen darf.] und leben die
Friedens=Richter in grosser Auctorität, cum plenipotentia, das
Böse mit Ernst abzustraffen.

Die 74. Frage.[45]

Was man gutes und Rechtschaffenes darunter finde?

R. Die gegebene Gesetze sind dermassen gut, daß es nicht
wohl übel zugehen kan, es sey dann, daß böse Regenten
ins Land kämen, die da Gott und der Wahrheit feind wären.
[Man kann sich die wahl bey Lesung Englischer Gesetz
Bücher machen, nur das die Volks-Menge bey uns nicht
so gross und dahero so leicht keine Unterschleif gegen die
guten Gesetze geschehen kan. Es sey denn das böse Regenten wären.]

[44] Question LXV in MSS.
[45] Question LXVI in MSS.

The 73rd Question.

Under what regulations do the present Colonies stand, and how are they governed by the Magistrates? How is evil combated and the good encouraged?

———

THE present colonies are governed according to the English law, which pleases me greatly as there is ample freedom, and no absolute tyranny. I also know that according to the instruction of the Justices of the Peace in England, they have a greater authority in *publico* to punish the evil than any preacher dare assume publicly.

———

The 74th Question.

What is to be found amongst them, that is good and righteous?

———

THE given laws are good to such a degree that matters can hardly go amiss, be it then that bad rulers come into the country, who would be a foe to God and Truth.

By reading the English law books, one can make his own selection, bearing in mind that the population with us is not nearly so great, and therefore the beneficent laws cannot readily be circumvented, it be then that the rulers are bad.

Die 75. Fräge.[46]

Wie die Städte in Pensylvanien alle heissen? wie weit
sie von einander gelegen? an was für Flüssen? was
sie für Gemächlichkeit haben? wie viel Häuser
und Einwohner? ob in einer jeden Stadt
unterschiedliche Secten und Religionen?
oder [in einige] nur eine?

R. [**D**ER nahme der meisten städte in Pennsylvanien
sind diese] In Pensylvania ist die Haupt=Stadt
Philadelphia, ohngefehr von [1300 bis] 1400. Häusern beste=
hend, [davon die Hälfte reguläre und von Steinen und Kalk
wohl aufgeführte Häuser sind] Puclingthon aus [ohnge-
fehr] 400. Häusern [bestehend] Chester 200. Neu Castle
300. Salem [mehr denn] 100. Germantown [ohngefehr
über 50.] 150. Franckfurt [40] 45. Barby 40. Rathnor 40.
Elisabethtown 45. [Darby, Ratnor, Elizabethtown in jeglicher ohngefehr 40 bis 50] welches [Guelsche oder Gualli-
sche Städte und noch andere Dörfer von einzeln Häuser um
sich haben] Grallische Städte sind, wo benebens noch andere
Dörffer mit einzelen Häusern anzutreffen. Die [Fals] Pfaltz
ist mit Holländern und Widertauffern bewohnt. Passagin und
Christina sind Schwedische Oerter [und viele einzelne *Plantagien* auf und nieder der *River Skulkil* und *Christinakil*
haben] Es gibt auch viel einzele Plantagien von 4. 5. 6. und
mehr Häusern beysammen. [Hiernächst sind auch viele Dörfer und einzelene *Plantagien* hin und wieder von 2, 3, 4,
5, 6, etc. Häusern beisamen]

[46] Question LXVII in MSS.

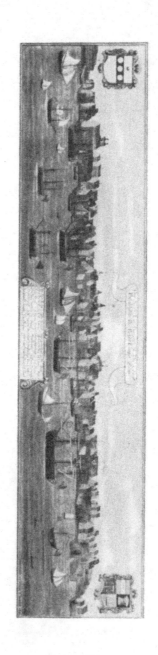

CURIEUSE NACHRICHT VON PENNSYLVANIA.

THE SOUHEAST PROSPECT OF THE CITY OF PHILADELPHIA.
BY PETER COOPER, PAINTER.
THE OLDEST VIEW OF THE CITY KNOWN. PAINTED ABOUT THE YEAR 1717.
PHOTOGRAPHED FROM ORIGINAL PAINTING IN THE PHILADELPHIA LIBRARY. COPYRIGHT 1901.

The 75th Question.

How are all the towns in Pennsylvania named, and
how far are they apart, upon what rivers and
their conveniences, the number of houses
and inhabitants, and if in every town
there are divers sects and religions, or only one?

THE names of the chief towns in Pennsylvania are :
the City of Philadelphia, of about thirteen to fourteen hundred houses, of which number about one half are
regularly built of stone and lime ; [65] Porlington [66] consists
of about 400 houses; Chester, of about 200; New Castle,
300; Salem, more than 100; Germantown, about over
50; Frankfort 40; Darby, Radnor, Elizabethtown each
about 40 to 50, which are Welsh or Gaelic towns, with
sundry villages of scattered houses. The Falls [67] is settled
by many Hollanders and Anabaptists. Passajim [68] and
Christina are settlements of the Swedes, who have many
separate plantations on the rivers Schuylkill and Christinakil. Hereabout there are also many villages and
single settlements of 2, 3, 4, 5, 6, etc., houses together.
The sects and religious parties live among one another.
Of the rivers, see Question LII, together with other no-
table conditions in the future.

Die Secten und Religions=Partheyen leben mit [unter] ein=
ander, doch sind an einem Ort von der einen mehr als von der
andern. Von Flüssen vide Supra. [wie oben Ques. LII
gedacht nebst anderen Notabeln umständen künftig]

Die 76. Frage.[47]

[Wohin und auf was weise oder] Wormit am meisten
in Pensylvania gehandelt werde?

R. Alls Pensylvania mit Mehl, Zwybacken, starck Bier,
Butter, Käse, geräuchert und gesalzen Fleisch, gesalzene
Fische, ꝛc. fahren gen Barbados, Jamaica und Antego. Von
dar bringen sie zurück Weine, Rummi oder Brandwein, Syrupp,
Zucker, Pfeffer, Ingber, Lemonen, Gewürtz, Baumwoll, Negros.
In Engelland führen sie allerhand Häute und Felle, samt köst=
lichem Peltzwercke, bringen hinwiederumb Kleider und allerhand
Haußrath und Handwercks3eug.
[Der meiste Handel von Pennsylvanien geschicht nach
Permudus, *Barbados*, *Jamaica* und *Antecho*, wohin ge-
schiffet wird Mehl, Zwieback, Starck Bier, Butter, Käse,
geräuchurt und gesaltzen Fleisch, gesaltzene Fische etc.
Von dannen kompt hinwieder zu uns Weine von *Mathera*
und anderen Orten *Rum* das ist Brandetwein von Zucker
Rieth distilliret, Syrup, Zucker, Indigo, *Jamaica* Pfeffer,
Ingber, Lemonen, Melonen und andere dergleichen
Früchte und Gewürtzer. Item Baumwolle, Leder, *Negros*
oder Sclaven und dergleichen. Hiernechst handelt man
nach *Marienland*, *Virginien*, *Carolina*, *Providents*. Item,
nach *Neu-jork*, *Neu-England*, *Neu-Fundland* oder *Terra*

47 Question LXVIII in MSS.

The 76th Question.

The commerce of Pennsylvania, whereto, in what manner, and where in does it consist?

THE chief commerce of Pennsylvania is with the Bermudas, Barbadoes, Jamaica and Antigua, to which are shipped flour, ship-biscuit strong beer, butter, cheese, smoked and salted meats, salt fish, etc. In return, there comes to us wine from Madeira and other places, rum, that is brandy made from sugar cane, distilled syrup, sugar, indigo, Jamaica pepper, ginger, lemons, melons, and similar fruits and spices; likewise cotton, hides, negroes and slaves and the like. Besides, we trade with Maryland, Virginia, Carolina, and Providence, likewise with New York, New England, Newfoundland and Terra Nova, sending the same merchandize and receiving for them money or such products as they have there, namely tobacco, salted fish, whale oil, tar, hemp, flax, boards, beef and pork, etc. For England, vessels are loaded with skins, peltries and tobacco, and in return bring us household stuffs, and clothing, and occasionally also men servants and maids, who are chiefly Irish and Scotch.

nova mit eben denselbigen dingen, und bekompt vor seine
Wahren Geld oder andere Wahren als da sind; Toback,
Saltzfisch, Thran, Ther, Hanf, Flachs, Bretter, Eisen,
Syder oder Äpfelthrank, Fleisch in Tonnen, Rind oder
Schweinefleisch etc. Nach Engeland gehen Schiffe mit
Fell-Peltzerey und Toback beladen und bringen uns hin-
wieder Hausrath und Kleidung, zuweilen auch Knechte
und Mägde in *specie* Irländer und Schottländer.]

Die 77. Frage.[48]

**Auf was Weise man sich dessen zu einem Vortheil in Er-
weiterung des Reichs Gottes bedienen könne?**

R. **DAS Reich Gottes erweitert sich von sich selbst, wann es
durch Reichthumb der Kauffleute geschehen solte, so würde
es schlecht darmit hergehen, doch laugne ich nicht ab, daß nicht der
gütige Gott durch fromme und erleuchtete Christen viel gutes
ausrichten könne.**
[Es ist sonst leichter nach dem Ausspruch der Wahrheit, dass ein Kamel ins Nadelöhr eingehe, denn dass ein
Reicher ins Himmelreich komme. So möchte es auch
wohl leichter sein, dass sich das Reich Gottes aus seinen
eigenen Mitteln erweiterte, denn dass es auf den Reichthumb der Kaufleute, die es so geschwind und mit Haufen
gewinnen können, darauf warten und sich davon aufhelfen
lassen solle; doch leugne ich nicht, dass recht fromme
Christliche Gemüther viel guts bey Gelegenheit der Handlung ausrichten können, aber sie sind dünne gesäet, doch
sind derselben und können sie hier vor mich am besten
aufs neue umsehen nach den Töchtern der Menschen mann

[48] Question LXIX in MSS.

The 77th Question.

In what manner could this be made to serve to the advantage and extention of the kingdom of God?

THE kingdom of God extendeth itself, if it were to depend upon the riches of merchants, it would fare badly therewith, though I do not deny that the good Lord could effect much good through devout and enlightened Christians.

According to the truthful saying it is far easier "for a camel to go through the eye of a needle than for a rich man to enter into the kingdom of God." Thus the Kingdom of God might be more easily extended by its own expedients than by waiting on the pleasure or depending upon the wealth of the merchants, who can so rapidly amass it. Yet I do not deny that some right devout Christian souls could effect much good as the opportunity presents itself in their traffic. But such are sowed sparsely, although there are some who can here best answer for me, if anything like this should come to pass. To be competent, the naturalization as well as citizenship should be acquired in London; thus one or two *nomine multorum* or even an entire German colony could trade free-handed, according to the English law, with London, Bristol, New York and all royal plantations enumerated in Question LXVIII. Internal commerce every one pursues in his own province as well as he can.

antworten. Doch wenn etwas dergleichen geschehen soll, so hinlänglicht seyn könte, so müsste man die *naturalisation* zugleich mit dem Bürger-Recht in London Annehmen und also einer oder zwei *nomine multorum* oder gar einer ganzen Deutschen *Colonie* auss freyer Hand nach dem englischen Recht nach *London*, *Bristol*, *Newyork* und alle Königlichen *numero quaest. LXIIX.* berührte Plantagen handeln. Inländischen Handel treibet ein jeder in seiner Province so guth er kann.]

Die 78. Frage.[49]

Wann dardurch dem Reiche Gottes einiger Schade geschihet, ob nicht solchem auf einige Weise zu begegnen?

R. **Wie groß der Schade sey,** [und seyn könne] **in dieser letztern Grundsuppen der Welt, lasset sich dahero** [abnehmen] **judiciren, weil Gottes Wort und die Religion selbst zu einem verdammlichen Commercio gemacht worden ist.** [dass man den Schaden ins allgemeine zu helfen nicht absehen kan. Was will man denn nun von der Handlung sagen, weil darinnen ein oder zwei Menschen, wass die *Essential* oder Grund-*Reguln* betrifft, nichts ändern können. Doch wie die Creatur, wider ihren Willen der Eitelkeit unterworfen ist auf Hoffnung so möchten fromme Kaufleute solcher-gestalt auch im ausseren ihren Dienst gar füglich und in Gottes willen anwenden und selbst durch fleissiges Gebeth und gute Betrachtung ihrem Gewissen satisfaction geben und ihrer Hand-Arbeit, dass sie im Seegen gethan sey beweisen können.] **Da kan man fast keine Hülffe absehen,**

The 78th Question.

Should anything arise thereby prejudicial to the Kingdom of God, could it not be overcome
in some manner?

———

HOW extensive the damage is or might be in these
our final dregs [67] of the world, may be judged by
the fact that even God's Holy Word and religion itself
have been turned into a damnable traffic, so that in general
it is hard to see how the damage can be repaired. Now
what shall we say about an action where one or two persons
cannot alter what concerns the essentials or fundamental
law? But as the creature is subjected against its will to
vanity in hope, so might devout merchants of such calibre
so dispose their services in outward matters as to apply
them unto the will of God, and personally by diligent
prayer and self-contemplation of conscience give satisfaction, and by their labor prove that it was done in the spirit.

und muß allhier die Creatur wider ihren Willen der Eitelkeit
unterworffen ſeyn, biß daß der Liebe Gott auff unſer fleiſſiges
Gebet nach ſeinem Wohlgefallen denen lieben Seinigen Rettung
verſchaffet.

Die 79. Frage.[50]

Was von Particulier Hiſtorien bekannt iſt, ſo ſich mit
denen Wilden zugetragen?

R. Wo Gott das Leben friſtet, ſo will ich mich bey meinem
retour in Pensylvanien alles genau erkundigen, was
ſich bey 50. und 60. Jahren zwiſchen denen Wilden, Schweden,
Teutſchen, Holl= und Engelländern zugetragen, und ſo dann auff
dieſe Frage antworten.
[Hierzu mangelt mir die Zeit und wolte wünschen, dass
das was ich hin und wieder bei guten Freunden erzehlet,
aufgeschrieben wäre. Wo ich lebe so will ich mich mit
Gottes Hülfe bey meinen guten Freunden *legitimiren* und
auch der *quaest. LXXII.* genug thun mit Bericht aller
particularen, so diese 50 bis 60 jahre hiero zwischen den
Wilden, Schweden, Holländern und Engländern passiret,
ordentlich zusammenfassen.]

[50] Question LXXI in MSS.

The 79th Question.

What particular histories are known concerning the savages?

FOR this the time is lacking, and I would that what I had related here and there to good friends were written out. If I live and with the help of the Lord, I expect to prove my intentions with my good friends and thereby do full justice to Question LXXII in all particulars, and gather what has thus far taken place for the past 50 or 60 years between the savages and the Swedes, Hollanders and English.

QUESTION LXXII IN FRANCKE MSS.

Likewise traditions current among the settlers themselves who have come to America, which would give some good reminiscences of accounts thereof.

THIS question is No. LXXII in the original list of questions by Francke, vide p. 56 supra it does not appear to have been answered in either the manuscript or printed version.

Die 80. Frage.[51]

Was von dem Zustande anderer Länder und Insuln in America bekannt ist, sonderlich wegen des Zustands Christlicher Religion? [Imprimis quoad statum Religionis Christianae?

R. [UNTER andern ist dieses kürtzlich das Vornehmste] Virginia ist allein unmittelbar, durch den Revers des Königs, als ein freyes Königreich vorbehalten, und kan an keinen Herren absolut verkaufft oder vergeben werden, deßwegen auch desselben Gräntzen nit limitirt sind usque ad mare pacificum. [Sondern wo die anderen *provincien* aufhören, da ist *Virginien* biss an das *mare dela Nord* oder *pacificum*, davon wie weit es dahin sey, wir noch keine Nachricht haben, vermuthlich dass es viel 100 Meilen in *specie* nach Nordwest und West. Die übrigen *Provincien* sind meistentheils an *Lords* oder grosse Herren von Engeland ihrer *meriten* halber übergeben. Doch *limitate*, dass sie Vasallen vom Königreich und die Englische Kirche als die Haupt Säule des Königs-reiches ihrer Freyheit nach dero hergebrachten *Statutis praetendiret*.] Pensylvania ist an Printz William Penn vom König in Engelland übergeben, doch limitate als Vasallen vom Königreiche. In Pensylvanien werden alle Secten, ausser Juden, und Atheisten, die Christum offenbahr verlaugnen [nicht allein] gedultet. [Sondern es wird denselben auch ihr freies *exercitium Religionis* vergönnet, und werden dabei *publica autoritate* ungestöret geschützet, ja sie werden von allerhand Arth Leuten *ad officia publica admittiret*, und wird von keinen mehr gefordert, als dass er nur ein guter Bürger sey. Dieses ist in

51 Question LXXII in MSS.

The 80th Question.

What is known about the condition of the other countries and islands in America: *imprimis quoad statum religionis christianæ.*

AMONG the others this[67] one is of late the foremost. Virginia is the only one retained by the King's immediate declaration as a free kingdom, and cannot be sold nor granted to any lord absolutely. Therefore its boundaries are unlimited, and wherever another province ends, it becomes Virginia, until the Polar and Pacific Ocean is reached. How far this is, we as yet have no advice. Presumably it is many hundreds of miles towards the northwest and west. The other provinces are chiefly granted to the lords or great men of England for different merits, though they are so limited as to be vassals to the crown; and the established church, as the chief pillar of the kingdom, maintains the freedom of its pretentions according to the statute.

In Pennsylvania all sects except the Jews and such as absolutely deny Christianity, are not only countenanced, but they are granted the free exercise of their religion and are undisturbed and protected by the public authorities. Yea, all sorts and conditions are admitted to public office, and nothing is asked any more of one, than that he shall be a good citizen.

This is different in Maryland, Virginia, New England, etc., for there the sects are countenanced, as are the Jews; but the public exercise of their religion is forbidden, yet in private they may conduct their worship undisturbed.

Marienland, Virginien, Neu England etc. nicht also, den allda duldet man die Secten wol, wie auch die Juden, aber das letztere ist ihnen versaget, doch mögen sie *privatim* ungestöret ihren Gottesdienst halten.]

Die 81. Frage.

Wie in Pensylvania mit einigem Capital ein Profit zu machen?

R. Jch will hier ein Project entwerffen, wie man ein Capital zu geschwinden Nutz, und auch zu Gottes Ehre, und des Christenthumbs Aufnahme anlegen könne:

1. Jch lege an 4000. Thaler an an Kauffmanns-Waare, davon sollen nothdürfftig unterhalten werden 8. Personen uff 2. Jahr lang.
2. Sollen gekaufft werden 1000. Aecker Landes.
3. Darauf soll gebauet werden die nothdürfftige Unterhaltung für Haußhaltung, Menschen und Viehe.
4. Zu kauffen 2. Stuten 1. Hengst 2. Pflug-Pferde 2. Ochsen.
5. 6. Kühe mit Kälbern oder trächtig.
6. 4. Säu mit Jungen oder trächtig.
7. Nothwendiges Geschirr sambt derer continuirlichen Verbesserung.

Dieses ausgelegte Capital der 4000. Thaler soll in 5. Jahren ertragen.

1. Den Sold und recompens für 2. Præceptores oder Professores Publicos.
2. Den Sold für 2. Knechte und 2. Mägde in der Hauß- und Feld-Arbeit.

The 81st Question.

How to make a profit with some capital in Pennsylvania.

ᚻERE I will map out a project how a capital may be placed advantageously to give quickr eturns, and at the same time revert to God's glory and the advancement of Christianity.

(1) I invest 4000 thaler in merchandize, wherefrom shall be economically supported eight persons for a term of two years:

(2) There shall be bought 1000 acres of land.

(3) Buildings shall be erected thereon for the mere support of the households, people and cattle.

(4) To buy 2 brood mares, 1 stallion, 2 plough horses, 2 oxen.

(5) 6 cows with calf or gravid.

(6) 4 sows with litter or pig.

(7) Necessary implements together with continual betterments.

This invested capital of 4000 thaler shall yield within five years:

---

(1) The salary and recompense for two preceptors or public teachers.

(2) The salary for the servants and two maids for work in house and field.

(3) Stipend for a preacher, who not as a lord over the people, but as a servant of Jesus Christ and the congregation teaches *auctoritate publica* in the church and in

3. Den Sold eines Predigers, der nicht als ein Herr des Volcks, sondern als ein Knecht JEsu Christi, und der Kirchen-Glieder auctoritatepublica in der Kirchen lehre, und in Gesellschaft 4. alter verständiger frommer Männer, als Mit-Aeltisten richte, darneben Gottes Wort als Gottes Wort in Lauterkeit predige ohne Menschen-Satzung und anathematisirende Formen.

Uber obige Besoldungen verbleibet am Vorrath noch so viel übrig, daß man

1. Gelegenheit hat, ohne Schaden Gastfrey zu seyn.
2. Frembdlinge und Wilde zu beherbergen.
3. Schue, Kleider und Haußgeräthe zu verschaffen.
4. Sein gantzes Haußwesen mit aller Nothdurfft zu versehen.

AUSFÜHRLICHER PLAN IM HALLESCHEN MANUSCRIPT.

conjunction with four old intelligent devout men directs, at the same time preaching God's word as God's word in all its purity, without any human statutes and anathemizing forms.

———

In addition to above charges there remains on hand enough, that we have :

———

(1) An opportunity to be hospitable without loss.
(2) To entertain strangers and savages.
(3) To provide shoes, clothes, household goods.
(4) To provide the whole household economically with all things necessary.

———

[The above published version of Falckner's project is a mere abstract of the original as fonnd in the Halle Manuscripts — the whole scheme is reproduced on the pages following the *Additamentum Questionum.*]

ADDITAMENTUM
QUÆSTIONUM.

Die 82. Frage.[52]
Woran in America Mangel sey?

R. **V**Ornehmlich [ist] an Menschen, und Handwerckern, der
übrige Mangel würde leicht zu ersetzen seyn.

Die 83. Frage.[53]
Woher man ein jedes nothwendiges Ding bekommen kan?

R. **A**US Engelland bekommt man das meiste, [nothdürftige]
doch wann America in seinen Stand erst wird gebracht
seyn, so wird es sich mit denen meisten Dingen selbst helffen kön=
nen, die Bergwercke und Manufacturen wollen Geld haben [darzu
wir noch erst Vorbereitung machen und unseren Acker
erweitern] daran wir der Zeit nicht gedencken dörffen, biß das
Ackerwerck erweitert, und jährliche Unterhalt zur Gebühr werden
eingerichtet worden seyn. [was von einer jeglichen *Provinz*
zu erhalten sey, wird aus der vorigen *quaest.* Beantwortung
zu ersehen sein]

52 Question LXXIII in MSS.
53 Question LXXIV in MSS.

ADDITAMENTUM QUÆSTIONUM.

The 82d Question.

Whereof is there a deficiency in America?

THE chief deficiency consists in settlers and mechanics; the other deficiencies wherever they exist are easily supplied.

The 83d Question.

Where are all necessary things to be obtained?

FROM England we receive the most necessary articles, yet as soon as America gets into its proper position, it will be able to supply itself with almost all things. Mines and manufactories need money; therefore we shall yet have to make preparations and extend our acres. What is to be obtained from the other provinces in North America will be seen by my answer to a previous question.[72]

Die 84. Frage.[54]

Was die Europäer aus Engelland und Holland vornehm=
lich mitzunehmen haben?

***

R. DAVON wird die Lista ehistens von Herrn Heinrich Peter=
son in Bremen folgen.

***

Die 85. Frage.[55]

Was man sonderlich aus Engelland und Holland zur Lei=
bes= und Gesundheit=Pflege mit zu Schiffe zu neh=
men haben?

***

R. [Hausrath und Kleidung] Von Artzney=Mitteln die=
jenige Materialia, die ein jeglicher in seiner Hauß=
Apothek nöthig erachtet. [wie er etwas] An Gewürtz, Corde=
mümmelein, Neglein, Muscaten, und Muscaten=Blumen, Saff=
ran, Zimmet, Rosinen, [und dergleichen mit sich nehmen
mag, ihn solches wohl zu statten kommen, Er kan es auch
theuer wieder verkauffen. Item. Eine gute Büchse voll]
Mithridat, Thiriac, [Krebsaugen und rothe *Corallen*] 2c.
worvon man jenseits im Verkauffen guten profit machen kan.

54 Question LXXV in MSS.
55 Question LXXVI in MSS.

The 84th Question.

What the Europeans have chiefly to bring with them
from England and Holland.

———

HERE the list of Heinrich Petersen, of Bremen, will
shortly follow.

[Vide page 239.]

———

The 85th Question.

What should be taken on shipboard from Holland
and England for the special benefit of
the body and health.

———

CLOTHING and household goods; of medicines,
such remedies as each person judges necessary
for his medicine chest. If they wish to take any spices
the following will prove to be of advantage: cardamon
seeds, cloves, mace, saffron, cinnamon, nutmegs, currants,
raisins and the like. They can also be sold here at a large
profit; also a good small canister of mithridate[73] and
Theriaca,[74] crab's eyes and red coral.

Die 86. Frage.[56]

Bey weme man sich bey seiner Ankunft in America am
ersten anzumelden habe?

R. Bey seinen nechsten [bekanten] Freunden, und bey dem
Gouvernatore des Landes, und [nur dieses] ist [all
hier] zu wissen, daß einer, der in das Land kommet, frey seyn
mag, wo er will, wann er auch schon keinen Freund hätte, [nie-
mand fraget ihn und kein Verdacht oder *rumor* entstehet
seinet halben] es ist ihme auch alles frey, gleich nachzuthun,
was er siehet einen andern [einwohnern] thun.

Die 87. Frage.[57]

Ob auch einem Europäer frey stehe mit seinem in America erworbenem Gut, wieder nach seinem Belieben
[zurück zu kehren] heraus zu reisen?

R. Ja wann er will, nur muß ers 4. Wochen zuvor [öffent-
lich melden, ehe er wegreiset] andeuten, damit, wo
jemand etwas gegen ihn zu sagen hätte, er es thun möge. Und
damit er ungehindert reisen möge, so bekommt er einen Paßport
von dem Guovernement. [Dieser *Passport*, wenn er mit des
Königs Siegel bedrückt ist, muss der *Gouverneur* selbst
solches in vollem Gewehr und Rüstung und unter aufge-
richtete standarte verrichten.]

[56] Question LXXVII in MSS.
[57] Question LXXVIII in MSS.

The 86th Question.

To whom must one report firstly upon his arrival in America?

TO his well-known friends. How further to conduct oneself has already been set forth in former answers. This, however, is to be remarked, that those who come into this country are at liberty, if they so desire, even if they have no friends. No one questions them, and no suspicion or rumor arises upon their account. They are entirely at liberty to do the same as they see other inhabitants do.

The 87th Question.

Is a European at liberty to return at his pleasure, with such property as he acquired in America?

YES, if he wants to only he must give public notice of his intention four weeks in advance, so as to advise any who have claims against him. Then he can depart and go without hindrance; a passport is granted him by the government. If this passport has the royal seal attached, the governor must salute it in full regimentals and armour and under a raised standard.

Die 88. Frage.[58]

An was für Handwercksleuten es daselbst am meisten fehle?

———

R. **ES könnten allerhand Gattungen Arbeit genug bekommen, dann diejenige, so bereits da sind, haben mehr zu thun, als sie wohl verrichten können.** Vide plura supra quaest 2. [Es mangelt in so weit noch an allen, ob schon welche da sind, so haben sie doch mehr zu thun, als sie wohl verrichten können. Die vornehmsten aber hab ich in der Beantwortung der Andern *quaest.* schon angeführet]

———

Die 89. Frage.[59]

Wie es die Wilden bey dem Begräbnus ihrer Todten halten?

———

R. [DIESES habe ich zwar selbst nicht gesehen, doch ist mir glaubwürdig erzählet] **Sie machen ein Loch, oder Grab, darein sie den Todten lähnen, dem geben sie etwas Essen mit, und nebst demjenigen, was er auf Erden sonders lieb gehabt, auch seinen Bogen uad Pfeile, oder eine Flinte, damit er auf dem Weege jagen könne, dieweil sie glauben, er reise nun gegen dem warmen oder kalten Lande, nachdem er nehmlich gut oder böse gelebt hat. Das grab wird oben mit Höltzern** [oder Rinden] **und Gras zugedecket, und so dann Erde darauf gehäuffet. Bey demselben befindet sich die Frau mit den Kindern** [und anverwandten] **öffters ein, und klagen, haben auch eine gewisse**

———

[58] Question LXXIX in MSS.
[59] Question LXXX in MSS.

The 88th Question.

What manner of handicraftsmen are mostly wanting?

———

THERE is a deficiency thus far of all kinds. Although many are already here, they have more to do than they can well attend to. But the most important I have already enumerated in previous answers.

———

The 89th Question.

How do the savages act at the burial of their dead?

———

THIS I have never witnessed, though I have received trustworthy information that they make a hole or grave in which they lean [75] the dead and also place some food, together with his bow and arrows or a rifle, so that he can follow the chase upon the way, as they believe he now journeys merely toward a warm or cold country, according to the kind of life led here. The grave is covered with branches, bark and sod, upon which earth is heaped. The wife, children and relatives meet there to lament. They, however, set a certain length of time in which they want to think of and remember the dead. During this time they continually stir up the fresh earth on the grave, so that no grass can grow on it. When the time has expired, no one is permitted to mention the name of the dead, since he is now to be forgotten, or else they get very angry.

Zeit, wie lange sie der Todten gedencken wollen, in welcher Zeit sie die Erde auf dem Grabe immer umbrühren, damit kein Gras darauf wachse. Wann die Zeit aus ist, darff niemand des Verstorbenen Nahmen mehr nennen, weil sie ihn nun vergessen, sonst werden sie ungehalten.

Die 90. Frage.[60]

Ob der Eydschwur bey ihnen bräuchlich? wie solches geschehe? und gegen wen sie schwören?

R. DJESES weiß ich nicht, ob sie schwören, [und] oder wie sie schwören?

Die 91. Frage.[61]

Ob die Wilden den siebenden Tag heiligen? und wie sie solchen feyern?

R. NEIN, ich [redete einstens mit einem bey Gelegenheit davon] fragte einst einen, warumb er am Sontag arbeitete? Der gab mir zur Antwort! Er müsse am Sontag so wohl essen, als am andern Tage, darumb müste er jagen, wann er aber schon etwas hätte, dann hielte er Sonntag. Die Saccaracca (oder die Französische Indianer) welche die Franzosen zu ihrem Glauben sollen bekehret haben, die halten den Sontag. Welches die andern Indianer zu ihrem Vortheil gebrauchen, und sie an demselben feindlich überfallen, und tödten. [Dahin wieder die *Frantzosen* zur *Pænitenz* vor ihrer Sünden den wilden auflegen, so viel von denen andern zu tödten oder

---

[60] Question LXXXI in MSS.
[61] Question LXXXII in MSS.

The 90th Question.

Is an oath customary amongst them, and how is such administered, and by whom?

I CANNOT say whether they administer any oath, or how they do it.

The 91st Question.

Whether the savages sanctify the seventh day, and how they observe it.

NO. Upon one occasion I spoke to one as the opportunity offered and his answer was, "that he must eat upon the Sabbath, as upon every other day, and therefore he must go on the chase; but that if he were already provided, then he would keep the Sabbath.[76]

The *Saccaracco* or French Indians whom the French claim to have converted to their faith, keep the Sabbath, which the other savages take advantage of, and attack and kill them upon that day. The French in return to appease them, advise them, as a penance for their sins, to kill or bring in as many of their enemies as possible.

gefangen einzubringen] Da hingegen diese uff die andere
Täge in der Wochen dahin trachten, ihren erlittenen Schaden zu
revangiren, und der Feinde wiederumb so viel zu tödten.

Die 92. Frage.[62]

Ob bey denen Wilden nicht einiges Verlangen nach der
wahren Erkanntnus Gottes zu spühren, wann diejenigen, so ihre Sprache verstehen, mit ihnen
reden?

R. DAS kan ich nicht sagen, weilen ich [so gar viel nicht
mit ihnen *conversieret* und] ihrer Sprache noch [so]
nicht mächtig [gewesen] bin. Es heisset bey ihnen: Ignoti
nulla cupido, [oder man müste sie auf gut Spanisch bekeh-
ren, oder auf Frantzösich formalisiren, nach dem Stats
intresse.] ich hoffe [dass die überbliebenen von ihren Volk
zu seiner Zeit dem äusserlichen Vorhof der Christenheit
mit ein verleibet und denen christlichen Einwohnern daselbst
von jeglicher nation einige zur Ausbeute geschenket und
zum monument werden anvertrauet werden] aber doch, daß
sie noch dem Schos Christi werden einverleibet werden, ohne
Spanische Forcirung.

[62] Question LXXXIII in MSS.

The 92d Question.

Whether there is evident among the savages some
longing after a true knowledge of God, when
such as speak their language talk
with them.

THAT I cannot answer, as I have not conversed
much with them, for I am not yet master of their
language. With them it signifies *ignoti nulla cupido*, or
we would have to convert them in the old Spanish manner,
or according to the French formula, according to the interest of the State. I trust that the remainder of these people
may in due time be ushered into the outer court of Christianity, and be distributed for their profit among the
Christian inhabitants of various nations, and become as
a monument to whom they were intrusted.

Die 93. Frage. [63]

Was die Wilden von der Auferstehung der Todten hal=
ten und glauben?

R. Sie glauben kein rechtes formales Sterben, so können sie
auch kein rechtes Concept von der Auferstehung haben,
weilen sie ins warme, oder ins kalte Land ihre Hoffnung einrich=
ten. [besiehe die LXXX Frage]

Die 94. Frage. [64]

Was die Wilden [Leute] für Gewehr führen?

R. Bogen, Pfeile, Röhre, Flinten, Messer, kleine Hand=
Beyler, Pulver, Kugeln, Dunst.

Die 95. Frage. [65]

Ob nicht einige Philosophi oder Gelehrte [Leute] unter
den Wilden? worinn sie sich üben? und ob sie auch
den Lauff des Himmels observiren?

R. Ihre Philosophia bestehet in der Astrologia, in deme
sie nicht allein der Sternen Nahmen wissen, sondern auch
das Wetter accurat zuvorher anzeigen können. [Es kam eins-
mahls ein wilder in der Nacht im Holtze zu mir und meinen

[63] Question LXXXIV in MSS.
[64] Question LXXXV in MSS.
[65] Question LXXXVI in MSS.

The 93d Question.

What the savages hold and believe of the resurrection of the dead.

THEY do not believe in any formal death, consequently they cannot have any true conception of a resurrection, as they introduce the departed into a warm or a cold country. Vide the eightieth question.

The 94th Question.

What sort of arms do the savages carry?

BOWS and arrows, guns, knives and small axes.

The 95th Question.

Whether there be not some philosophers or learned men amongst the savages; what they practice and whether they observe the course of the heavens.

THEIR philosophy consists in astrology, wherein they not only have names for the stars, but can also foretell the weather accurately. Upon one occasion a savage came to me and my companions at night in the

Gefährten bey das Feuer, dieser sah den *Polar*-Stern an
und observirte daraus das es kalt werden würde, weil er so
sehr helle wäre, welches auch erfolgete, zugleichen erzeh-
lete er mir, wie er die Bewegung des *Polar*-Sterns in
einem hohlen Baum durch ein loch *observiret* und ange=
merket hätte, wie derselbe sich um das loch des Baumes
herumgedrehet hätte und bald halb, bald gantz wäre zu
sehen gewesen, und wäre am Himmel zu sehen gewesen
wie ein Tropfen Fett so auf dem Wasser schwimmet] **Jn=
gleichen stehet ihre Philosophia in der Physic von der Natur
und Eigenschafft der Thiere.** [einige wissen darin mehr als
andere, sonderlich] **Diejenige, so bey ihnen als Priester die
Opffer schlachten,** [welcher zugleich ihr *Medicus* ist. Insgemein sind sie gute *Galenici* und *Botanici* wiewohl ihre
Medicin nun mehro nicht zureichen will, weil sie sich nebst
den Kleidern auch unsere Lebensart annehmen] **sind die
besten Physici, und zugleich ihre** Medici, **nehmlich gute** Galenici.

Die 96. Frage.[66]

**Ob die Wilden auch einige Extraordinari Zeichen ob-
serviren und erkennen?**

R.   **J**A, [dergleichen ich aus der *historia* voriger Zei
abnehmen können] **sie wissen ex** Stella polari, & aliis
Syderibus, **das Gewitter vorzusagen.**

[66] Question LXXXVII in MSS.

woods,[77] as we were around the fire. He looked at the polar star, and observed therefrom that it would be cold, as the star was so bright, which came to pass. At the same time he told me how he observed the motion of the polar star through a hole in a hollow tree, and remarked how the same danced about[77] the hole in the tree, and could be seen now half, now wholly; and upon the sky it appeared like a drop of fat swimming upon the water.[77] Their philosophy in the physics consist likewise of nature and the properties of animals. Some know more about this than others, especially those who officiate as priests at their sacrifices, who are also their medicine men. Generally they are good Galenists and botanists. However, their remedies now fail to suffice, since they have adopted our clothing, together with out manner of living.[78]

The 96th Question.

Do the savages also observe any extraordinary phenomena and understand them?

YES; this I infer from accounts of former times. They know *ex stella polari* and *aliis syderibus* and can foretell storms.

Die 97. Frage. [67]

Ob nicht [unter ihnen auch einige] einige unter ihnen
ungewöhnliche Motus und [oder] Bewegungen [zu
spüren] haben? puta intrinsecus.

R. Ja man sagt, daß sie Offenbarungen von natürlichen Zu=
fällen haben, [wie auch aus der *historia* zu sehen]
und [so sagen sie auch] daß es ihnen geoffenbaret sey, daß
ihrer so viel sterben müssen, als viel unser hinein in ihr Land
kommen.

Wann es starcke Donnerwetter gibt, so fallen sie zur Erden,
und strecken die Armb von sich [werden öfters durch einen strahl
inwendig gerührt] und werden im Gesichte gantz blaß.

Die 98. Frage. [68]

Ob nicht unter denen mancherley Secten auch einige unge=
wöhnliche Bewegungen und Vorbotten der heran=
nahenden Gerichte Gottes zu spühren?

R. Ja, sehr viel, und zwar so, daß sie bey dem meisten gantz
Universal sind, und auf eine gantze Wiederbringung,
oder Wiedererneuerung aller Dinge zielen. Einige sind Particular [nachdem das Glass ist, so ist, das Gerichte, also]
dann nach dem der Prophet ist, so ist auch sein Zeugnuß, und muß
bißweilen auch ein unformlich scheinendes Ding, durch einen guten
Ausleger zur grossen Kunst und Weißheit ausgerechnet werden.

[67] Question LXXXVIII in MSS.
[68] Question LXXXIX in MSS.

The 97th Question.

Do not some among them perceive any motus
or agitation?

———

YES, it is said that they have manifestations of
natural events, which is also to be seen in the histories. Thus they say that it is revealed to them that as
many of them have to die as have come over of our kind.
During heavy thunder storms they fall flat upon the earth
and stretch out their arms away from the body, and are frequently moved inwardly by an ecstasy, and their faces pale.

———

The 98th Question.

If there be not some unusual manifestation perceived
among the sects of the harbinger of the
approaching millinium.

———

YES, a great deal; and indeed, so much so, that
with the majority it is universal, and they aim after
a complete restitution or restoration of all things.[79] Some
are particular; according as the glass, so is the reflection;
consequently as is the prophet so is also his testimony;
and occasionally a seeming dwarf but a good exponent,
will appear great in art and wisdom.

Die 99. Frage. [69]

Wie sich die sogenannten Geistlichen unter so mancherley
Secten in America aufführen, und so wohl unter
sich selbst, als gegen andere comportiren?

———

R. **D**IE so genannten Geistlichen verlieren unter uns gar sehr
das Monopolium, indeme man die Geistlichkeit nicht
[mehr] an die schwartze Kappe bindet, wiewohl an der andern
Seite wieder preccirt wird, daß man der Zungen zu viel an
einem Cörper machet, daß hernach viel Köche den Brey verderben.
So müssen sie sich auch der eigentlichen Herrschafft begeben, weilen
das Kirchen=Regiment [ob schon nicht bey allen] nicht bey
einem alleine, sondern bey vielen bestehet, [(Ich rede hier von
Secten)] und die Leute allhier insgemein so viel von der Kranck=
heit des Menschlichen Hertzens verstehen, daß sie wissen, wann auch
der Pfarrer kranck ist, (sonderlich wann er unordentlich kranck
wird) dahero dann auch, [der *Disput* oder zum wenigsten der
Vorwurf] die raisonirung mehr geführet wird über das Leben,
als über die Lehre des andern. Und weil ein jeder des Tages
Last und Hitze trägt, [darneben auch ein Nachtbahr den anderen im täglichen Umbgange und Hülfe nicht entbehren
kann, ob er schon andere *Religion* ist,] so lasset sichs nicht
Lärmen blasen, sondern die liebe Necessitas übertrifft alle Leges,
sonderlich bey denen, die in großmüthiger Stille seyn, und hoffen
alles annehmen zu können, wie es kommet.

[69] Question XC in MSS.

The 99th Question.

How the so-called ecclesiastics among the manifold
sects in America conduct themselves toward
each other, and how they comport
themselves toward others.

THE so-called ecclesiastics with us love their monop-
oly greatly, in so far that the ecclesiastics here are
not tied down to their black calotte. On the other hand,
however, it is *preccirt* that there are too many tongues for
one body, and that eventually too many cooks spoil the
broth, so they have to renounce any peculiar denomination,
as the church government consists of many, though not of
all (I allude here to the sects); and the people in general
know so much of the diseases of the human heart that they
can tell, not only when the preacher is sick, but when he
becomes disorderly. Upon this account there are more
disputations carried on, or at least reproaches, about their
life than about the law. As each day brings its own heat
and burden, and as one cannot dispense with the daily intercourse and help of his neighbor, though he be of a different religion, thus the time and sweet necessity surpasses all
laws, especially with such as maintain a magnanimous
silence, and hope to take all as it comes.

Die 100. Frage. [70]

Was vor Hoffnung sey, daß die mancherley Secten in eines zusammen tretten mögten?

R. DIESE, daß der HErr JEsus, in aller Gewissen König=lich wird proclamiren lassen, daß alle Menschen Lügner sind, damit ihme alles Fleisch schuldig sey, und den Baum des Erkanntnus Gutes und Böses fahren lasse, und sich unter den Friedliebenden Feigenbaum und Weinstock der Liebe mit Fleiß retirire, damit er das Judaisirende Dialogisiren, Opponiren, und Anathematisiren mit eins abandonire, und sich durch das Wort der Gedult vor der greulichen Stund der Versuchung, welche auf den gantzen Craiß des Erdbodens kommen wird, præseviren lasse. Wer nicht auf diese Weise will, der warte, biß daß alle in der Weite dieser Welt ausgebreitete Farben von sich selbst eine werden, welches doch ehender zu vermuthen, als daß so viel Köpffe, ausser GOtt, eines Sinnes werden sollen.

Die 101. Frage. [71]

Durch was für Mittel man die Wilden am meisten an sich ziehe?

R. WIE man die wilde Thiere, und Kinder an sich locket, und wie man eben dieselbe auf mancherley Art und Weise verschüchtern kan.

[70] Question in XCI MSS.
[71] QuestionXCII in MSS.

The 100th Question.

What hope is there that the divers sects may come
together as one?

THIS : viz., that the Lord Jesus will cause to be royally
proclaimed in every conscience that all men are
liars, so that all flesh may be indebted unto him, and re-
linquish the tree of knowledge of good and evil, and take
refuge under the fig tree and vine of charity; so that they
can at once abandon the judaizing dialogues, oppositions
and anathematization, and preserve themselves by the word
of patience from the horrible hour of temptation, which is
coming over the whole surface of the earth. They who
will not come in, in this manner, let them tarry until all
the different colors which are spread over the world become
as one by themselves, which is more probable than that so
many godless heads should become as one.

The 101st Question.

By what means can the savages best be drawn towards
us, and whereby are they mostly repelled?

JUST as wild beasts and children are won over unto us,
and in the same manifold ways that they are
repelled.

Die 102. Frage. [72]

Was die Wilden für Namen führen?

R. VOR Zeiten haben ſie ſich benennet mit denen Rahmen der wilden Thiere, als nach ihrer Sprache Fuchs, Wolff [Schlange, bunte Schlange, krumme Schlange etc.] rc. Jetzo aber gebrauchen ſie die Rahmen der Europäer, als Hannß, William, George, James, Antoni.

Die 103. Frage. [73]

Wann? und wie ſie ihren Kindern Rahmen geben?

R. NICHT alſobalden in ihrer Jugend, ſondern wenn ſie ziemlich erwachſen, und wann ſie unter ihren Kindern eines ruffen wollen, ehe ſie ihnen einen gewiſſen Rahmen geben, ſo ſchreyen ſie zu ihnen insgeſambt ein Hodo rc. Und wen ſie alsdann vermeinen, zu deme richten ſie ihr Angeſicht und Rede, und befehlen ihme.

Wormit ich dann meine Beantwortungen auf vorgelegte Fragen beſchlieſſe, und den günſtigen Leſer, nebſt mir, der Führung des Geiſtes Gottes wohl anbefehle, mit Wünſchung alles glücklichen und geſegneten Wohlergebens für den

Leib in dieſer Welt, und, für die Seele,
Freude und Troſt in Gott biß
an ſein

E N D E.

---

[72] Question XCIII in MSS.
[73] Question XCIV in MSS.

The 102nd Question.

What manner of names the savages have.

AMONG themselves, in former times, they used the names of wild animals in their own language, as Fox, Wolf, Snake, Harlequin Snake, Crooked Snake, etc. It is now their custom to use European names, such John, George, etc.

The 103rd Question.

When do they name their children?

NOT in their infancy, but after they are well grown. If they want to call one of their children before they have given him a certain name, they call to all with a Ho! Do! etc. When the one wanted sees them, they speak to him or give him their commands.

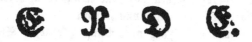

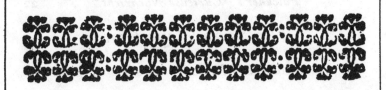

Wie in Pensylvania mit einigem Capital ein Profit zu machen?

Daniel Falckner's Project for founding a Community in Pennsylvania as set forth in the Halle Manuscript.

Weil ich der Zeit ermangele, so will ich von Zweyen projecten, davon ich oben *quaestione LIX.* gedacht eins machen, auß welchen in einem kurzen summarischen Begriff zu ersehen ist, theils wie man ein Capital zum geschwinden Nutzen daselbst anlegen, als auch die Ehre Gottes und Christliche Aufnahme der Jugend ohne große Weitlaufigkeit daselbst beförderen konne.

Ich nehme 4000 Rthlr. Dieselben lege ich an in solchen Kaufmans wahren, wie Beylage, so mit ehsten folgen soll, ausweisen wird. Diese 4000 Rthlr. sollen mir folgendes mit gottlicher Hülfe in Stand setzen.

1. Soll davon genommen werden nothdürftiger Unterhalt vor 8 Persohnen auf zwey Jahr.

2. Kan gekauft werden ungefehr 1000 Acker Landes oder mehr.

3. Kann gebauet werden vors erste zum nothdürftigen Behülf, Hausung vor Menschen, Vieh und Früchte.

4. Sind zu kaufen zwey gute Pflug Pferde, 2 Studen zur Zucht, 1 Reitpferd und 1 Paar Ochsen zur Arbeit.

5. Sechs Kühe mit Kälbern oder thrächtig.

HOW TO MAKE PROFIT WITH CAPITAL IN PENNSYLVANIA.

DANIEL FALCKNER'S PROJECT FOR FOUNDING A COMMUNITY IN PENNSYLVANIA AS SET FOR IN THE HALLE MANUSCRIPT.

AS I am falling short of time, I will make but one out of the two projects referred to in Question LIX, from which a short and concise conception may be obtained of how capital may be invested there, so as to bring quick returns, and at the same time how the glory of God and the christian affiliation of the youth may be furthered there without difficulty.

I will take say 4,000 Reichsthaler[80] and invest them in such merchandise according to the appended list. These 4,000 Thalers shall, with God's assistance, put me in possession of the following:

1. We will take enough therefrom necessary for the support of eight persons for a term of two years.

2. There may be purchased a thousand or more acres of land.

3. There may be built at first only the absolutely necessary shelter for man, beast and the crops.

6. Vier Säue mit jungen oder trächtig.

7. Nothdürftiges Geschirr und Geräthe mit verbesserung[des=
selben.

Dieses Capital also angeleget soll innerhalb 5 jahren abwerfen
wie folget.

1. Die jährliche Nothdürftige Versorgung dreyer Praeceptoren
oder Professoren davon ein jeder nach verflossenen 5 Jahren haben
soll.

1. 50 Acker Land erblich vor eine solche Station.

2. 30 Thaler am Gelde jährlich.

3. Eine Kuh mit dem Kalbe oder trächtig.

4. Ein gewißes an Bier, Fleisch, an Korn und dergleichen.

Diese Praeceptores sollen ihre Zeit nach richtiger eintheilung ein
jeglicher des Tages 4–5 Stunden in Unterrichtung der Jugend
nach einem compendiosen Weg auch wohl in der Muttersprache,
in artibus liberalibus informiren, darneben diejenigen so zu
äusserlicher Handarbeit nicht geschickt in linguis nationum etiam
Americanarum.   Durch den usum zu üben item in der Oeconomia
wie alle Dinge ordentlich und profitlich zu thun, zu unterrichten
und daß die Körper nicht aus Ermangelung der motion hypo=
chondrisch werden oder putreseiren, eine nach Vermögen befindliche
Arbeit in Garten=Werk, Unkraut aus zugäten und guten Saamen
zu pflantzen, item Bäume pflantzen, Schaafe pflegen, Fische fan=
gen, vor ihre Praeceptores Holtz machen und beyschaffen etc. und
dergleichen erträgliche Arbeit bey den übrigen müßigen Stunden.
Oder wenn etliche Lust hatten, eine gewisse Handthierung dabey
zu lernen so könte in der Colonie gehalten werden, ein Schuster,
ein Schneider, ein Zimmermann, ein Weber, ein Uhrmacher, ein
Kannen=Gießer, ein Goldschmied, ein Seiler, ein Rademacher,
ein Schmied, ein Schreiner, Drechsler, Mahler, Töpfer, und
dergl. damit ein jeglicher selbst wehlen könne, oder die Vorsteher
ihre Untergebene nach gut befinden anweisen können worzu sie sich
schicken.   Ein jeder solche Handwercks=Mann, der sich darzu will

4. To purchase two good plough horses, two mares for breeding, one saddle horse and one yoke of oxen for work.

5. Six cows with calves or gravid.

6. Four sows with young or pig.

7. Necessary harness and implements with repairs for same.

This capital invested in such manner should, within five years, yield profit as follows:

1. The necessary support of three preceptors or professors, whereof each should have received after the five years have elapsed:

    1. Fifty acres of land to be inheritable for such charge.

    2. Thirty Thalers in money yearly.

    3. A cow with calf or gravid.

    4. A certain stipend for beer, meat, grain and the like.

These preceptors shall so arrange their time, that each one may have from four to five hours every day to instruct the youth in some compendious way in their mother tongue, as well as to educate them in the liberal arts; and let them instruct such as show no inclination for outward handicraft in *linguis nationum etiam Americanarum.* Likewise instruct them practically in economy, how to do all things properly and profitably; teach them that their bodies should not become hypochodriac or putrescent from lack of exercise; but work them during the idle hours, according to their capacity in garden work, pulling weeds, planting seeds, likewise setting out trees, tending sheep, catching fish, gathering and chopping wood, etc., for their preceptors, and similar profitable work during their idle hours.

Or if some incline to learn certain trades, the colony could keep a cobbler, tailor, carpenter, weaver, watchmaker, pewterer, goldsmith, ropemaker, wheelwright,

gebrauchen lassen, soll haben 10 Acker Landes, will er mehr haben
so sollen deswegen, die nächstliegenden Ländereyen angekaufet
werden und ihnen vor Bezahlung auf gewisse termine zugelassen
werden, so viel er will. Darneben sollen seine Kinder das selbige
Recht der Auferziehung vor anderen geniessen und bey seinem
Absterben vor dieselbigen und die Wittwe Sorge getragen wer=
den. Die lehrlinge was sie bey müssigen Stunden nach genaue=
ster einsicht, eines jeglichen Arbeiten, soll zu einer Summa ge=
rechnet seyn, davon der Meister den Vorschuß vor Materialien
abziehen soll, das übrige in 2 gleiche Theile getheilet, davon der
eine Theil dem meister pro labore, der andere der cassa pro com-
muni bono heimfallen soll. Die Eintheilung der Zeit könnte
alsdann gemachet werden, nur das man Morgens, Mittags und
Abends, ehe man schlafen gehet, eine Stunde zum Gebeth, Bibel
lesen und singen vor alle und jede ausgesetzet seyn mußte, darzu
ein Zeichen gegeben werden konte, das derjenige welcher aus recht
erheblicher Ursachen nicht persönlich erscheinen kan doch an seinem
Orth mit beystimmen möge dem Verlangen und Lob Bekänntniß
seiner Freunde und Mitbürger.

2. Soll gedachtes Capital auch abwerfen die anschaffung und
Erhaltung zweyer Knechte und Mägde.

3. Eine Prediger der nicht als ein Herr des Volkes sondern
als ein Knecht Jesu Christi und der Kirchen=Glieder autoritate
publica in der Kirchen lehre und in Gesellschaft vier alter ver=
ständigen und frommen Männern als mit Eltesten richte, und was
ungleich ist, schlichte, darneben Gottes Wort in Lauterkeit predige
ohne Menschen Satzung und anathematisirende Formuln; soll
haben 40 Rthlr. und etwas gewisses an Fleisch und andere pro=
vision. Das übrige seines Unterhalts muß man auf andere
Weise suchen, und das man die Kosten fürs erste erspare, so soll
die Aufsicht und Rechnung einer der Schul Collegen führen und
dasselbige Jahr eine Stunde weniger Schularbeit täglich haben
die rechnung aber soll er im Beyseyn der anderen Collegen der 4

blacksmith, cabinet-maker, turner, painter, potter, etc., so that every one could make his own selection. Or the wardens could advise their dependents to such trade as in their judgment they are best fitted.

Every one of such handicrafts men, who lends himself thereto, shall have ten acres of land; if he wants more, additional adjacent land shall be bought and given to him, as much as he wants, the payment to be made at convenient times. In addition his children shall enjoy equal rights and privileges of education with the others. And in case of his death, care is to be taken of the same and the widow provided for. Apprentices who, during idle hours, perform any work, shall, after careful examination of each one's work, be credited with the same, from which the master is to deduct the money advanced for material; the remainder is to be divided into two equal parts, one of which goes to the master of the apprentice, the other part into the treasury of the community. Any division of the day may be made, provided one hour is set apart, morning, noon and night before going to sleep, for prayer, bible reading and singing, for which a signal must be given, so that such as may be prevented by weighty reasons from being present may yet at their station join in with the devotions and commendations or praise of their friends and fellow citizens.

2. The said capital should also yield enough to obtain and keep two menservants and maids.

3. A preacher, who does not seek to be a lord over the people, but rather who, as an humble servant of Jesus Christ and the members of his church, shall be a public exponent[81] of the doctrines of the church, and administer justice in fellowship with four aged, intelligent and devout men as presbyters; equalize that which is inconsistent, and

Eltesten sambet zweyer nach dem Englischen Recht legitimirten Friedens Richtern abgelegt werden.

§ 4. Soll bey Anwachs und vermehrung des Viehes eine gewiße Zahl gesetzet werden, was sich durch Gottes Seegen drüber vermehret soll zur caßa vor ankommende oder auswartig Armen aufbehalten oder im Gelde bey geleget werden.

Aus diesen folgen nun mehr-andere nutzbarkeiten darunter folgende nicht die geringsten als.

(1) Die Gelegenheit ohne Schaden gastfrey zu seyn.

(2) Frembdlinge und Wilden aufzunehmen und zu beherbergen.

(3) Schuh, Kleider, Geräthe u. s. f. ohne Unkosten verbeßern zu laßen.

(4) Sein Volk wohl zu regieren und mit aller Nothdürfftigkeit ohne Weitläuffigkeit und Kosten durch sie selbst und ihre Kinder zu versehen.

Beylage so in quaestiom 84 erwahnet wird.

at the same time preach God's Word in its purity, without any additions of human institutions or anathematizing for muleas. He shall receive 40 Thaler and a certain stipend for meat and other provisions. The balance of his support must be sought in some other manner. That the expenses may be kept down for the present, the oversight and accounts shall be kept by one of the school masters, for which purpose he shall be required to teach one hour less daily. The accounts shall be rendered in the presence of the other masters, the four presbyters, together with two Justices of the Peace, commissioned according to the English law.

4. A certain number shall be agreed upon for the increase and multiplication of the cattle, and whatever increase there be over and above such number, by the blessing of God, shall be set apart for the benefit of the arriving or outward resident poor, or else turned into money for the same purpose.

Upon these follow sundry other useful purposes, among which the following are not the least : —

1. The opportunity to extend hospitality without prejudice.

2. To entertain strangers and Indians, and accomodate them with lodgings.

3. Shoes, clothing, implements, etc., to be repaired free of cost.

4. To govern the people well, supply them with all necessaries without any ceremony through themselves and their children.

LYSTA DERJENIGEN WAHREN, SO IN PENSYLVANIEN
ANGENEHM SIND, NACH H. FALCKNER SEINEM
BEHALT AUFGEZEICHNET.

Holländische Osnabrüggische Leinwand; davon man erst in
Engelland Nachricht einholen muß, ob man es in Holland einla=
den und wie hoch die Accis ist.

Holländisch weißer Zwirn, allerhand Band.

Verroische gewalckte Strümpfe, Bremer Beylacken wegen der
Accis zu vernehmen in Engelland.

Einschlag=Messer, einige gute Scheermesser.

Bohrer vor 2 Daumen zu der Nagel Bohrer, allerhand Feilen,
Breitbeil und Düpel, Meissel.

Schnitz=Messer die nicht zu klein sind vor häußlichen und Zimer=
leute Gebrauch, einige vor Böttiger zu gebrauchen.

Grabe=Scheit, Schaufeln, Mist= und Korn=Gabeln in Engel=
land zu kaufen.

It. Sicheln, Sensen und dergl.

Große Seegen eiserne und stälerne Hand=Seegen, die im Rücken nicht Ungleich und nicht zu schwach sind.

Handbeil, allerhand Meis=sel

nicht von der Art welche die Zim=merleute gebrauchen Zimmer=Holtz ein zuschneiden sondern die weitge=setzt, vollkommen lang, und da die Zähne die Halfte — einer, die an=dere Hälfte — der andern weg stehet.

(238)

List of such Goods, as are Acceptable in Pennsylvania, according to the remembrance of Herr Falckner.

DUTCH and Osnaburggish linen, about which one must first inquire from England, whether it can be shipped in Holland and how high the tariff is.

White Holland thread, all kinds of tape.

Veronese felted stockings, Bremen bed sheets, are on account of the tariff to be obtained in England.

Clasp knife and several good razors.

Augurs, from two inches down to the gimlet, all sorts of files. Broad axe and hoes, drills.

Draw knives not too small for domestic as well as carpenters use. Several for use of coopers.

Spades, shovels, dung and grain forks to be purchased in England, also sickles, scythes, etc.

Large saws, iron and steel handsaws, which are uniform in the back are and not too light. Not of the sort used by carpenters to cut boards, but the wide set, ample long sort, wherein one half of the teeth are set to cut one way, and the other half the reverse.

Hatchets and all sorts of chisels.

Smith, and ordinary hammers, etc.

Schmid= und gemeine Hämmer etc. Wieder und brecheisen oder Kuhfüße.

Eisen, das keine Brandrisse hat, und guten Stahl Flemisch, Eiserne Ofen.

Eiserne Stücker, die schon zu Pflugscharen geschmiedet, ohne die eisernen Stangen, die daran sind und von den Kleinsten, welche in Engelland am besten zu haben, das 100 ohngefehr vor 15 Pf. sterling.

Eisserne Potte aber wenig eisserne Kessel.

Kupfer, gelb und roth, mehr kleine als große Kessel.

Kupferne verzinnte Pötgens und Thee= oder Coffe=Potte.

It. Kannen vor 1/2 Kannen Maaß.

Englisch Kersey und allerhand gering wollen zeug vor Unter= futter einiges in modesten Farben vor Frauen Ober=Kleider, einiges rothes vor Unter Kleider und sprenglichtes vor Kinder.

Die Mittelsort von Lacken, grau, braun nnd dergl. modesten Farben, wenig schwartze Blanketes und Madratzen.

It. einige bunte Hals= und Nase Tücher, gedruckten Carbun oder Leinen vor Kinder, Zwilch und Pargen vor Bett=Zeug.

Gewürtz	Corinthen, Muscaten, Safran, Cordemum, Maces, etc. Große Rosinen.

Eine Küste mit Glaß und Bley, wie es in Engelland verkauft wird, um Fenster zu machen.

Kraut und Loth, keine Kugeln sondern ungegossen Bley, oder Tauben, Enten, Gänse und schweren Hagel.

Eine Familie so da auf dem Lande zu bauen und zu leben ge= denket, soll sich, wo ihr der liebe Gott das Vermögen gegeben, mit Kleider und Betten versehen und denn in ein Faß, welches an der Accise in London in generalen Benennung der Nahmen

Barb-bolts, crow bars, or crooked bars. Iron that has no flaws and good Flemish steel, iron stoves.

Iron blanks already forged for plow shares, without the iron rods, and of the smallest to be had in England, one hundred costing about £15 sterling. Iron pots, but few iron kettles.

Copper, both yellow and red, more small than large kettles.

Tinned copper pots, also tea and coffee pots, likewise tankards of half quart size.

English kersey, and all kinds of cheap woolen stuffs for linings; some in modest colors for women's outside garments; some red for underclothes, and spotted for children.

The middle sorts of bed sheets, grey, brown and of similar modest colors, a few black blankets and matresses. Likewise some bright colored neck and handkerchiefs. Printed cotton or linen for children, ticking and fustian [82] for bed clothes.

Spices, currants, nutmegs, safran, cardemon, mace, etc., large raisins.

A case of glass and leads as they are sold in England to make windows.

Powder and shot, no bullets, but bar lead, pidgeon, duck, goose and heavy shot.

A family that expects to live in the country and cultivate the land should, if the good Lord hath blessed them with means to supply themselves with clothes and bedding, these should be put into a barrel, which could be entered at the customs in London as necessary household stuff, without (itemizing) among which can be packed two or three good hatchets, a broad axe, one or two hoes, three or four iron wedges, several iron rings, a door knocker, plough wheels and such.[83]

von Sachen (nicht oben die Numer) als nothdürftiger Haußrath angegeben werden kann einpacken wie folget. 2 oder 3 gute Hand=Beile, eine breite Axt, 1 oder 2 Düssel, 3 oder 4 eiserne Keile, einige eiserne Ringe an Klopfer, Pflugräder und dergl. zu legen.

1. par Holtz=Feilen und ein par andere dito Eiserne Beschläge vor einen Schwengel am Pflug oder Wagen.

It. 1 oder 2 mittelmässige Ketten, um schwer Bau=Holtz anf den Schlitten zu schleppen, als bey uns die Ketten sind, damit die Räder am Wagen gehemmt werden, wenn es berg ab gehet. Eine kleinere von der Art.

2. par Ketten von Pferde=Geschirr, Ketten vor Kühe daran feste zu machen, und eine kurtze Ketten vor allerhand Nothfall, in sonderheit an die eiserne Egge fest zu machen.

20 oder 30 eiserne Zähne vor einer Egge, die Zähne müssen sehr stark sein, sonst bengen sie sich im neuen Lande, wenn sie durch die Wurtzeln gehen, etwas gehärtet, doch nicht zu viel und von guter Länge. Pflugschaar ist dort besser nach der Landes=Art zu verfertigen, doch mag man die Form, davon wir auf dem andern Blatt gedacht beylegen.

100. oder nach Gelegenheit mehr Schindel, Clapport und Latten, Nagel, Haus, Stall und Scheuer zu machen, Thür=Angel=Hacken, Ketteln, Schlosser, Bäuder, an die Fenster und Fenster=Laden.

Ein gut lang Schnitzmesser vor Schindel zu schaaen.

Bohrer 2 Daumen, 1 Daumen, 1/2 Daumen und Nagel=Bohrer vor 2 oder 3 Arten.

Ein gut Stück Eisen und Stahl vor eine Axt nach dortiger landesart zu machen.

Ein par gute Hand=Seegen und eine große Holtz=Seege.

1 eiserner Morsel und einen kleinen messinger oder von Ertz.

1. Mistgabel, Misthacken, Heugabel, 2 Grabscheit, Schaufel und dergl.

1. par feine Mark=Sensen oder Hochteutsche Korn und Große Sensen.

One pair of wood rasps and a pair of other files.

Irons for a swingletree for plough or wagon, likewise one or two medium-sized chains to drag heavy timbers upon the sled, same kind as we use as a break to our wagon wheels when going down hill, also a lighter one of the same sort.

Two pairs of chains for horse-harness, cow chains, and a short chain for any kind of emergency, especially to fasten to an iron harrow.

Twenty or thirty iron teeth for a harrow, the teeth must be very strong, else they bend in the newly broken ground when they strike the roots. They should be tempered, but not too much, and be of a good length.

Ploughshares, it is best to have them made there according to the manner of the country, although one may also take such as are indicated upon the previous page. A hundred or more shingles according to opportunity. Clapboards and laths, nails for house, stable and barn, door hinges, pickaxes, hasps and staples, locks, hinges and clasps, locks, hinges and bands for windows and shutters.

A good long drawknife for shaving shingles, augers of the size of two thumbs, one thumb and one half a thumb's breadth, also gimlets of two or three sizes.

A good blank of iron or steel to make an axe according to the American kind.

A pair of good hand saws and a large wood saw.

An iron mortar and a small one of brass or bronze.

One dung fork, manure drag, pitchfork, two spades, shovel and the like.

One pair of fine briar scythes or good German grain and heavy scythes.

A goodly quantity of pig lead, several padlocks. When several families calculate to go far inland and lay out a

Ein gut Theil ungegossen Bley, einige Vorlege Schlösser. Wenn einige Familien tief ins Land einen neuen Platz anzulegen gedacht, müssen sie bedacht seyn auf ein par gute Mühlsteine und was eisern Werk zu einer Mühle gehöret.

Sollte sich auch ein Müller finden, der eine Beutel-Mühle, wie man in Ober-Teutschland hat, verfertigen wolte, dabey er zugleich Gersten, Weitzen, Haber, Speltz, Reis schelen könnte, der solte sehr angenehm sein.

Ein par Distillirer um Pfirschen, Apfel und Korn zu distilliren, wie es alda gebräuchlich.

Gute lange Flinten, die den Hagel weit und wohl schießen.

Einige Pistolen, Steigbügel, Gaffeln, Vorgeschirr die stark sind.

SOME

P R O P O S A L S

For a Second Settlement in the

Province of Pennsilvania.

W Hereas I did about nine Years paſt, propound the ſelling of ſeveral *Parts*, or *Shares* of Land, upon that ſide of the *Province of Pennſylvania*, next *Delaware-River*, and ſetting out of a Place upon it for the building of a *City*, by the name of *Philadelphia* ; and that divers Perſons cloſed with thoſe Propoſals, who, by their ingenuity, induſtry and charge, have advanced that *City*, from a Wood, to a good forwardneſs of Building (there being *above* One Thouſand Houſes finiſht *in it*);and that the ſeveral *Plantations* and *Towns* begun upon the Land, bought by thoſe firſt Undertakers, are alſo in a proſperous way of Improvement and Inlargement (inſomuch as laſt Year, *ten Sail of Ships were fraighted there, with the growth of the Province* for *Barbados, Jamaica,* &c. Beſides what came directly for this Kingdom) It is now my purpoſe to make another *Settlement*, upon the River of *Suſquehannagh*, that runs into the Bay of *Cheſapeake*,and bears about fifty Miles *Weſt* from the River *Delaware*,as appears by the *Common Maps of the Engliſh* Dominion in *America*. There I deſign to lay out a *Plat* for the building of another *City*, in the moſt then to pay but *one ſhilling* per annum for every hundred *Acres* forever. And further, I do promiſe to agree with every Purchaſer that ſhall be willing to treat with me between this and next Spring, upon all ſuch reaſonable conditions, as ſhall be thought neceſſary for their accommodation, intending, if God pleaſe, to return with what ſpeed I can, and my Family with me, in order to our future reſidence.

To conclude, that which particularly recommends this *Settlement*, is the known Goodneſs of the Soyle, and Scituation of the Land, which is high & not Mountainous ; alſo the Pleaſantneſs, and Largneſs of the River, being clear and not rapid, and broader then the *Thames* at London-bridge many Miles above the place deſigned for this *Settlement* ; and runs (as we are told by the *Indians*) *quite through the Province*, into which many fair Rivers empty themſelves. The ſorts of *Timber* that grow there, are chiefly *Oake, Aſh, Cheſnut, Walnut, Cedar,* and *Poplar.* The native *Fruits* are *Pawpaws, Grapes, Mulberys, Cheſnuts,* and ſeveral ſorts of *Walnuts.* There are likewiſe great quantities of *Deer,*

convenient place for communication with the former Plantations on the *East*, which by Land, is as good as done already, a Way being laid out between the two Rivers very exactly and conveniently, at least three years ago; and which will not be hard to do by Water, by the benefit of the River *Soakill*; for a *Branch* of that River lies near a *Branch* that runs into *Sufquehannagh* River, and is the *Common Courfe* of the *Indians* with their *Skins* and *Furrs* into our parts, and to the Provinces of *Eaft* and *Weft-Jerfy*, and *New-York*, from the *Weft* and *North-Weft* parts of the *Continent* from whence they bring them.

And I do also intend that every one who shall be a *Purchaffer* in this propoſed *Settlement*, shall have a proportionable *Lot* in the ſaid *City* to build a Houſe or Houſes upon; which *Town-Ground*, and the *Shares* of Land that ſhall be bought of me, ſhall be delivered clear of all *Indian* pretentions; for it is been my way from the firſt, to purchaſe their Title from them, and ſo ſettle with their conſent.

The *Shares* I diſpoſe of, contain each *Five* Thouſand *Acres*, for 100 *l.* and for greater or leſſer quantities, after that rate; The Acre of that Province is according to the Statute of the 33th of *Edw.* And no Acknowledgement or *Quit-Rent* ſhall be paid by the Purchaſers till five years after a Settlement be made upon their Lands, and that only according to the quantity of Acres ſo taken up and ſeated, and not otherwiſe; and only

and eſpecially *Elks*, which are much bigger than our *Red Deer*, and uſe that River in Herds. And *Fiſh* there is of divers ſorts, and very large and good, and in great plenty.

But that which recommends both this *Settlement* in particular, and the Province in general, is a late *Patent* obtained by divers Eminent Lords and Gentlemen *for that Land that lies North of* Pennſylvania *up to the* 45th Degree and an half, becauſe their *Traffick* and *Intercourſe* will be chiefly through Pennſylvania, which lies between that Province and the Sea. We have alſo the comfort of being the *Center* of all the Engliſh Colonies upon the *Continent* of *America*, as they lie from the *North-Eaſt parts of New-England to the moſt Southerly parts of Carolina*, being above 1000 Miles upon the Coaſt.

If any Perſons pleaſe to apply themſelves to me by Letters in relation to this affair, they may direct them to Robert Neſs Scrivener in *Lumber-Street* in *London* for *Philip Ford*, and ſuitable anſwers will be returned by the firſt opportunity. There are alſo *Inſtructions* printed for information of ſuch as intend to go, or ſend Servants, or Families thither, which way they may proceed with moſt *Eaſe* and *Advantages*, both here and there, in reference to *Paſſage*, *Goods*, *Utenſils*, *Building*, *Husbandry*, *Stock*, *Subſiſtance*, *Traffick*, &c. *being the effect of their Expence and Experience that have ſeen the fruit of their Labours.*

William Penn.

Printed and Sold by *Andrew Sowle*, at the *Crooked-Billet* in *Holloway-Lane*, *Shoreditch*, 1690.

new place, they must consider a run of good mill stones, and the iron work required for a mill.

If there should also be found a miller, who has a bolting mill, such as are used in north Germany and is willing to set it up, so that at the same time he could hull barley, wheat, oats, spelt [84] and rice it would be very acceptable.

A couple of distillers, to distill from peaches, apples and grain as is customary there.

Good long guns that will throw shot far and well. Several holsters, stirups, throat-halliards and strong led-harness.

APPENDIX.

1. God's Word and Grace.

2. Psalm CXXIII.—

Unto thee lift I up mine eyes, O thou that dwellest in the heavens.

Behold, as the eyes of servants *look* unto the hand of their masters, *and* as the eyes of the maiden unto the hand of her mistress; so our eyes wait upon the Lord our God, until that he have mercy upon us.

Have mercy upon us, O Lord, have mercy upon us; for we are exceedingly filled with contempt.

Our soul is exceedingly filled with the scorning of those that are at ease *and* with the contempt of the proud.

3. Prov. 21 : 25. The desire of the slothful killeth him : for his hands refuse to labor.

4. Many shall be purified, and made white, and tried; but the wicked shall do wickedly; and none of the wicked shall understand : but the wise shall understand. Daniel XXII., 10.

5. *Der Englische Schweiss*, a certain epidemic fever prevalent in England during the fifteenth and sixteenth centuries.

6. Unless it be that one has found ships at nearer ports intending to sail for America. Ed., 1702.

7. William Penn's original plan for the settlement and development of his province was to place the capital city upon the banks of the Susquehanna and not upon the Delaware, a scheme to which Penn clung tenaciously for a number of years after the settlement of the province. Daniel Falckner who was more or less intimately acquainted with Penn and his plans for the settlement of his province, evidently supposed that the chief city would be founded on the banks of the Susquehanna, in accordance with Penn's proposals for a "second settlement in the province of Pennsylvania," published in London 1690. A copy of this exceedingly scarce document is preserved in the Archives of the American Philosophical Society at Philadelphia and is here reproduced in fac-simile. For a complete account of this scheme, see paper by the present writer on "Penn's City on the Susquehanna," read before the Lancaster County Historical Society and published in Proceedings, Vol. II., pp. 223–238.

8. Chesapeake Bay.

9. The river of the Moose Deer.

10. This evidently alludes to the troublous times incident to the Spanish succession.

11. *i. e.*, without excessive drinking, etc.

12. To previously dispose his thoughts and mind toward quiet and sedate subjects. Ed. 1702.

13. Zwieback — a Biscuit rusk, or sweet spiced bread toasted.

14. Cider, Apple Jack [apple brandy], etc.

15. This comparison is very curious, and one which the writer has never before seen brought out in connection with our early history. By a comparison of several old German Almanacs with local ones of similar date, Falck-

ner is virtually verified, and shown to be a close observer
and student.   Thus in Pennsylvania the shortest day has 9 hours, 8
minutes.   The sun rises at 7.26 A. M. and sets 4.34 P. M.
In Germany the corresponding day has 7 hours, 34
minutes, as the sun rises 8.11 A. M., sets 3.45 P. M.
The longest day in Germany has 16 hours, 45 minutes,
the sun rises 3.39 A. M., sets 8.24 P. M. The corresponding day in Pennsylvania, June 22, has 14 hours, 50
minutes.   Sun rises 4.34 A. M., sets 7.26 P. M.

16. All kinds of German Grain and Indian Corn of different kinds.   Ed. 1702.

17. *Mespilus germanica.*

18. The black or sour gum tree is evidently the species
alluded to.

19. *Guaiacum or lignum vitae.*

20. Cf. Edition, 1702.

21. Leggings, hunting shirts and moccasins.

22. *Cannabis sativa.*

23. *Quibus ceremoniis.*

24. *Polygami.*

25. And all support themselves by hunting.   Edition
1702.

27. Wampum, beads formed of the interior parts of
shells, such as the great clam, the pearl oyster or venus
shell.   Were strung on threads, and formerly used among
the American Indians as currency, and worn also in neck-
laces, belts, etc.   The beads were either black, dark pur-
ple, or white, the last being the *wampum* proper.

28. *Haar Zöpfe.*

29. *Principia generalia religionis.*

FALCKNER.

30. Evidently alluding to other members of the community of German Pietists on the Wissahickon.

31. The aborigines of the West Indies and South America are meant here.

32. The Dutch navigators who first discovered this group of islands called them the Flemish Islands.

33. The expedition of Prince Madog ab Owen Gwynedd, about the year 1170, is here alluded to. The discovery and settlement of America by the Welsh is based upon an account in a history of Wales, written by Caradoc, of Llancarvan, Glaumorganshire, in the British language, to which were added from time to time remarkable occur rences registered in the Abbies of Conway and Strat Flur. The best copy of these registers was taken by Guttun Owen a Bard about the year 1480. Cynfrig ab Gronow also mentions this event about the same time.

The story is "that upon the death of Owen Gwynedd, Prince of North Wales, about the year 1169, several of his children contended for his dominions: that Madog, one of his sons, perceiving his native country engaged, or on the eve of being engaged, in a civil war, thought it best to try his fortune in some foreign climes. Leaving North Wales in a very unsettled state, he sailed with a few ships which he had fitted up and manned for that purpose to the westward, leaving Ireland to the north. He came at length to an unknown country where most things appeared to him new and uncustomary, and the manners of the natives far different from what he had seen in Europe. Madog having viewed the fertility and pleasantness of the country, left the most part of those he had taken with him behind (according to Sir Thomas Herbert 120 souls) and returned to Wales. Upon his arrival he described to his friends what an extensive land he had met with, void of

any inhabitants, whilst they employed themselves, and all their skill to supplant one another, for only a ragged portion of rocks and mountains. Accordingly, having prevailed with considerable numbers to accompany him to that country he sailed báck with ten ships and bid adiew to his native land." After which Madoc and his followers were never more heard of.

Alexander von Humboldt, who thoroughly investigated the various reports and stories of Welsh traditions and language which were said to still be current among the American Indians, says:

"The deepest obscurity still shrouds everthing connected with the voyage of the Welsh chief Madoc, second son of Owen Guineth, to a great western land in 1170, and the connection of this event with the great Ireland of the Icelandic saga. In like manner the race of Celto-Americans, whom credulous travelers have professed to discover in many parts of the United States, have also disappeared since the establishment of an earnest and scientific ethnology, based not on accidental similarities of sound, but on grammatical forms and organic structure."

34. For a number of these various traditions here alluded to by Falckner and current in the province at that early day, see *An Enquiry into the Truth of the Tradition Concerning the Discovery of America by Prince Madog about the year 1170. By John Williams, LL.D., London, MDCCXCI.*

35. *Die rechte stange zu halten wüste.*

36. *Affen leibe* (*i. e.*, ape love.)

37. Hennepin.

38. Kriegsrecht.

39. *Werg*, from a short coarse hemp fiber.

40. N. B. in MSS.　Make a note of.

41. Note, the outer hull of the black walnut or hickory nut is evidently indicated here.

42. A kind of a crude Russian bath.

43. A curious tradition on this subject has been handed down from generation to generation in the writer's family, and told him when a child. The story comes from one of the family who was active in the French and Indian war, it states that the Indians always strove to make prisoners of the German soldiers or settlers, as they were specially desirable for their cannibalistic feasts, their meat being sweet and juicy. Their explanation for this choice was that the Quaker was to lean to eat, all skin and bone. The Irishman's meat was soaked with whiskey and useless and the Englishman's meat was tasteless and bloated. So when a robust German was captured he was tortured and killed, and dismembered, the parts being larded with fat pine splints and roasted over a slow fire.

44. Tomahawk.

45. Hematite.

46. Virtually a crude silo.

47. *Rothstürtzen, Grass-frosch, Rana fusca.*

48. *Hummel* — Bumblebee.

49. The guild of salt-makers of Halle, that so-called *Halloren*, are here meant. These workers in the salines of Halle in Saxony are a peculiar race or class supposed to be of Attic origin; and during Francke and Falckner's time were quite numerous. They are noted for their tall and robust physique, regular features, with high forehead and fine eyes, as well as their open and spirited character with a free and decorous deportment. They speak a special

dialect somewhat foreign to the German tongue and rich in peculiar expressions smacking of the saltery. They are also conspicuous for their devout and moral life. It was upon this account that they were singled out by the elder Francke for possible missionary work among the Indians. Since the introduction of steam apparatus, most of them have sought other occupations. The guild, however, which is entitled to certain rights and privileges, still keeps up all its ancient customs. Cf. Keferstein, Halle, 1843.

50. The long German mile is here meant. The location of this spring is not known to the annotator.

51. *Arndt wahres Christenthum* (Arndt's *True Christianity*) is here indicated. This is one of the greatest and most useful practical books produced by the Protestant church. An American edition in the German language was published by Benjamin Franklin and Johann Boehm in Philadelphia as early as 1751. The book was an octavo and contained 1,356 pages with 65 plates.

In 1765 Christopher Sauer printed at Germantown an edition of Arndt's *Paradisgärtlein*, a 24 mo. of 531 pages. Numbers of the various German editions of Arndt's works were brought from the Fatherland from the earliest days of our settlements, and were highly prized by the German settlers, who used the *True Christianity* for their spiritual guidance, especially when there was a lack of spiritual advisors in their vicinity.

52. Vide Sachse's *German Pietists*, Chapter, Reynier Jansen, pp. 100–108. Also *Pennsylvania Magazine of History and Biography*, Vol. IV., pp. 432–444 and *Early Printing in Pennsylvania*, by John William Wallace.

53. Sturgeon.

54. *Mustela* L.

55. Europe.

56. All goods and wares in that early day were transported on pack horses. It was not until many years after Falckner's time that wagon roads were made into the interior of the province.

57. America.

58. Europe.

59. *Schacherer*, a low pedlar, a term usually applied to pedlars who travel about the country on foot with a pack.

61. Allusion is evidently made here to Falckner's companions the German Pietists on the Wissahickon, who were living an exemplary and godly life there.

62. Germany.

64. Higher courts of the Province.

65. Bricks and mortar.

66. Burlington in New Jersey.

67. Falls of the Neshamany.

67 (note on page 197). *Letzten Grund-suppe.*

67 (note on page 207). Pennsylvania.

68. Passayunk.

71. Evidently in a sitting posture.

72. Compare with Question 76 supra.

73. An electuary used as an antidote against poisons.

74. One of the compounds of opium, also used against snake bites.

76. In this connection, see account of missionary efforts among the Indians of Rev. Jonas Aurem : Sachse's German Pietists, pp. 126 *et seq.;* Sachse's German Sectarians, Vol. II., p. 321 ; also remarkable reply of an Indian Chief, *ibid.*, p. 474.

254   *Curieuse Nachricht von Pennsylvania.*

77 (note on page 221). This is an exceedingly interesting piece of evidence, as it shows that Daniel Falckner did not confine himself to confines of the tabernacle on the Wissahickon or Germantown, but evidently explored the resources of the Colony as well.

77 (note on page 221). "*Herumgedrecht* does not appear to imply here a turning around so much as the irregular moving or dancing about, which would be seen when the air was unsteady. I should translate it *danced about*, which fits in exactly with what follows. For if he was watching the star through a small opening, this motion due to the unsteadiness of the air would sometimes carry it half or wholly out of sight."

Professor Charles L. Doolittle, Director of the Flower Astronomical observatory, connected with the University of Pennsylvania, when sending me above note on the *herumdrehung* of the Polar Star, adds the following comment upon Falckner's statement:

"I do not remember ever seeing before this a reference to a case where a wild North American Indian made any reference to the stars. They had reached the stage of development where they reckoned time by the moon's motion, but aside from the sun and moon the movements of the heavenly bodies received but little attention.

"An acquaintance with the planets and fixed stars is not found to any extent I believe, in case of primitive people, until they have reached a considerable degree of civilization; but a good deal of attention is likely to be given at a much earlier stage to atmospheric and other conditions which have to do with the weather.

"This appears to be what the Indian in this case has in mind. The unusual brightness of the star was of course

due to a very clear transparent state of the atmosphere, which meant to have been followed by colder weather. Thence the motion which was made evident by watching the star through a narrow opening was due to unsteadiness in the atmosphere.

"This extract does not make the point clear, whether in the present case the two went together, viz., unusual brightness, with an unsteady condition of atmosphere, but this is not at all an uncommon combination.

78. Compare question 40 supra. This is undoubtedly the list of Heinrich Peterson, of Bremen alluded to in Quesion 84 and the original of the short list following Question IV. in the printed version.

79. "The Restitution of all Things." The restitution of all the human family at some future time after the present life to sinless excellence and to divine favor. This is virtually the doctrine of the present universalists. It was also one of the chief dogmas of the mystical sects that flourished during the latter part of the seventeenth and the early years of the eighteenth centuries. Cf. Sachse's *German Pietists* and *Sectarians*.

80. The monetary unit of Northern Germany at that time. It is still used in the German Empire; its value is 3 marks or 71 cents in U. S. equivalent.

81. *Auctoritate publica.*

82. Fustian. This was a stout cloth of cotton and flax, and was noted for its durability and wear.

83. This is certainly the first published scheme for circumventing the custom house officials by emigrants to America. A desire which exists to the present day, and has been greatly elaborated by the tourist of to-day, until

the most drastic means have been called into play by the authorities.

84. *Spelt*. A cereal intermediate between wheat and barley but usually considered a hard grained variety of the former.   It was the chief cereal of Ancient Egypt being probably the rye of the time of Moses, of Greece and of the Roman Empire.   It is now cultivated mainly in Switzerland, in southern Germany and northern Spain under the name of German wheat.

Metalmark Books is a joint imprint of The Pennsylvania State University Press and the Office of Digital Scholarly Publishing at The Pennsylvania State University Libraries. The facsimile editions published under this imprint are reproductions of out-of-print, public domain works that hold a significant place in Pennsylvania's rich literary and cultural past. Metalmark editions are primarily reproduced from the University Libraries' extensive Pennsylvania collections and in cooperation with other state libraries. These volumes are available to the public for viewing online and can be ordered as print-on-demand paperbacks.

LIBRARY OF CONGRESS CATALOGING-IN-PUBLICATION DATA

Falckner, Daniel, b. 1666.
[Curieuse Nachricht von Pensylvania. English]
Falckner's Curieuse Nachricht von Pensylvania : the book that stimulated the great German immigration to Pennsylvania in the early years of the XVIII century / Daniel Falckner ; translated and annotated by Julius F. Sachse.
p.   cm.
Originally published: Philadelphia, 1905. Summary: "Reprint of a 1905 English translation of Daniel Falckner's Curieuse Nachricht von Pensylvania (1702). Includes the original German text on facing pages, and annotations comparing that text to a manuscript version"—Provided by publisher.
Includes bibliographical references and index.
ISBN 978-0-271-05384-4 (pbk. : alk. paper)
1. Pennsylvania—History—Colonial period,
ca. 1600–1775.
2. Pennsylvania—Social life and customs—To 1775.
3. Indians of North America—Pennsylvania—History.
4. Pennsylvania Dutch—History.
5. Germans—Pennsylvania—History.
6. Immigrants—Pennsylvania—History.
7. Germany—Emigration and immigration—History.
8. Pennsylvania—Emigration and immigration—History.
I. Sachse, Julius Friedrich, 1842–1919.
II. Falckner, Daniel, b. 1666. Falckner's Curieuse Nachricht von Pennsylvania.
III. Title.

F152.F17 2011
974.8'02—dc23
2011046806

Printed in the United States of America
Reprinted by The Pennsylvania State University Press, 2012
University Park, PA 16802-1003

The University Libraries at Penn State and the Penn State University Press, through the Office of Digital Scholarly Publishing, produced this volume to preserve the informational content of the original. In compliance with current copyright law, this reprint edition uses digital technology and is printed on paper that complies with the permanent Paper Standard issued by the National Information Standards Organization (ANSI Z39.48–1992).